Favourite Recipes
for your Baby & Toddler

annabel karmel

Favourite Recipes
for your **Baby** & **Toddler**

✽ a complete feeding programme
✽ over 80 recipes ✽ handy fill-in sections

LONDON, NEW YORK, MELBOURNE, MUNICH, AND DELHI

I dedicate this book to my children Nicholas, Lara, and Scarlett, and Oscar – my new baby (puppy)!

Project editor Helen Murray
Recipe editor Norma MacMillan
Designer Jo Grey
Project art editor Sara Kimmins
Senior art editor Peggy Sadler
Managing editors Esther Ripley and Penny Warren
Managing art editor Marianne Markham
Jacket designer Peggy Sadler
Production editor Ben Marcus
Production controller Wendy Penn
Creative technical support Sonia Charbonnier
Category publisher Peggy Vance
Allergy consultant Adam Fox
Nutritional consultant Rosan Meyer
Food styling Valerie Berry
Home economist Jayne Cross
Photographer Dave King
Photography art direction Luis Peral

First published as *Baby and Toddler Food Diary* in Great Britain in 2008 by Dorling Kindersley Limited
80 Strand, London WC2R 0RL. Penguin Group (UK)

Copyright © 2008 and 2011 Dorling Kindersley Limited
Text copyright © 2008 and 2011 Annabel Karmel

2 4 6 8 10 9 7 5 3 1
001 – 180738 – April/2011

A CIP catalogue record for this book is available from the British Library

ISBN: 978-1-4053-6657-1

Colour reproduced by MDP, Bath
Printed and bound by Leo Paper Group, China

Discover more at
www.dk.com

contents

foreword

It is often said that introducing good eating habits early on will set your little one up for life. Whether you see weaning as an exciting phase or are dreading the mess and the fuss, there is no doubt that weaning your baby is an important milestone for both of you.

It's only natural to approach weaning with some anxiety, after all, you want the best for your baby and there are so many things to think about. What is the right age to start? Is it OK to introduce fish at six months? Is it safe to heat your baby's food in a microwave? What about food allergies – are there some foods that should be avoided?

To ease you into the world of weaning, I have created this guide to help you through each stage, from what to eat when you are breastfeeding to the best first foods for your baby, and tasty meals to tempt fussy toddlers.

This is your personal food diary. Each recipe has a panel for you to record your baby or toddler's reaction and your own thoughts and variations to each recipe. There are meal planners for each age group, where I have suggested weekly menus, and also blank meal planners for you to fill in, so you can plan your child's diet for the week ahead. You, too, may have favourite recipes that you don't want to lose, so there are spaces within the book where you can write these in.

My career began after the death of my first child Natasha, who died from a rare viral infection, and my legacy to her was to write my first book, *The Complete Baby and Toddler Meal Planner*, which was also inspired by the persistent refusal of my second child Nicholas to eat. It soon became clear that there was a huge amount of confusion and many old wives' tales when it came to feeding babies and children, and so I decided to get to the truth of what were the best foods for young children, and even more importantly, find out how you could get children to enjoy eating these foods. I have since gone on to write another 21 books, which are sold all over the world.

The message I want to get across is that feeding children is about common sense and a mum's instinct. There are no rigid rules because every child is different. When to wean, what foods to avoid, and how much food to give your baby, for example, will depend very much on your own baby. My aim in this book is to empower you, by giving you all the information you need to make an informed choice, and dispel those old wives' tales.

I also aim to show you the importance of introducing as wide a range of food as possible to your baby from a young age. Babies eat very well in their first year, so take hold of this great window of opportunity – it will become much more difficult in the second year. Introducing your baby to a range of flavours will help to stop your child becoming a fussy eater later on, and is also believed to prevent allergies by sensitizing your child to certain foods.

So, get started – be empowered, experiment, and, most of all, have fun.

Annabel Karmel

early nutrition

Babies and toddlers have little tummies, so everything you serve them should be packed with the nutrients they need to become strong and healthy. What they eat forms the foundation of their health for years to come.

From birth until about six months, babies get everything they need from breast or formula milk. Babies grow and develop rapidly in the first years, so it's important to ensure they get a variety of nutrients in the form of carbohydrates, fat, protein, and vitamins and minerals (see chart, pages 12–13). Food must also meet energy (calorie) needs.

● carbohydrates

Carbohydrates are "energy" foods, and they provide your baby with his main source of fuel. Initially babies are weaned onto easy-to-digest refined carbohydrates like fortified cereals. When they are older they can be introduced to more complex carbohydrates, such as wholegrain breads, breakfast cereals and pastas, brown or wild rice, and other wholegrain products. These foods provide a range of nutrients (such as the B vitamins) as well as fibre, and have the advantage of breaking down slowly in your child's body and therefore keeping him satisfied for a longer period. Refined carbohydrates like cakes, sweet biscuits, and other sugary foods should be avoided as they supply few nutrients, but lots of "empty calories".

How much should you give every day?

✱ **3–5 servings of protein** 2–3 of which should be from meat, poultry, fish, or pulses, and 2 servings should be from dairy products. Combine your protein servings with carbohydrates and vegetables/fruit.

✱ **4–5 servings of healthy carbohydrates** Young babies need to have refined carbohydrates, but from about 1 year you can start to introduce complex carbohydrates.

✱ **5 servings of fruit and vegetables** Fruit and vegetables should form part of every meal and should also be provided as snacks between meals.

✱ **What is a serving?** There are no precise guidelines on portion sizes for children. You can estimate protein portions by looking at your child's hand: a portion of red meat, poultry, or pulses is the size of his palm; a fish portion is the size of his whole hand. Add carbohydrates and vegetables/fruit at least in equal amounts. If your child wants to eat more, increase carbohydrates and vegetables/fruit before increasing protein.

tips

Evidence suggests that food preferences are established early in life, so help your young baby to develop a taste for healthy foods

Give your child omega-rich food such as oily fish. Research suggests it improves children's behaviour and their ability to learn

Make sure your child has enough iron. Sources include red meats, oily fish, leafy green vegetables, and pulses

● protein

Protein is found in fish, lean meats, poultry, pulses (such as chickpeas, beans, and lentils), soya, dairy produce, eggs, and some wholegrains. It supplies your baby with the building blocks for growth and healthy development. It is also essential for maintaining body functions.

● fats

Fat is the most calorie-dense component of food and is necessary for growth and essential nutrients required for brain function. Fats also contain the vitamins A, D, and E, which are necessary for many body processes. When babies are breastfed, over 50 per cent of calories come from fat. Once babies are weaned, they still need more fats than adults to ensure that they grow and develop properly. Most important are the essential fatty acids, known as EFAs or "omega" oils, which are found in oily fish, nuts, seeds, olive and some vegetable oils, and avocados. These are important for brain and visual development and immune function. Research has shown that one of the EFAs from oily fish can improve children's behaviour and their ability to learn. Not all fats are the same, however, and some should be eaten in smaller quantities than others (see pages 10–11).

● water

Water is essential to the digestive process – both ensuring that there is adequate saliva for digestion and that waste products are eliminated properly. Without water, your baby's cells cannot build new tissue efficiently, toxic products build up in his bloodstream, and less oxygen and nutrients will be transported to his cells, all of which can leave him weak, tired, and at risk of illness.

● fibre

Fibre has a host of roles in your baby's body, which encourage it to function properly. Fibre literally acts as a broom, clearing away debris from the digestive tract and keeping it healthy. It also adds bulk to your baby's diet, which contributes to healthy bowel function. In addition, fibre stimulates the flow of saliva, which protects teeth and encourages healthy digestion. Fibre is found in almost all fruits, vegetables, and grains – one reason these foods are so important to health.

● prebiotics

Prebiotics are non-digestible food ingredients that aid absorption of nutrients, reduce intestinal infections, and improve immunity. Good sources are oats, wheatgerm, onions, garlic, and leeks.

healthy eating

Creating a healthy diet for your child is easier than you may think. Giving your child balanced, healthy meals will set a good example for him later on in life. Here are a few key tips to remember.

● go for five a day

Fruit and vegetables are essential for healthy babies and children. They offer a wide range of vitamins, minerals, fibre, some proteins and complex carbohydrates, and are naturally low in or free from unhealthy fat. It's easy to purée a few different fruits and vegetables together for your baby, and make sure you offer your child fruit as snacks and alongside every meal to ensure that he's getting enough.

● offer variety

If your child eats the same things day after day, chances are he'll be missing out on a few key nutrients. Brightly coloured fruits and vegetables have very different nutrients to leafy greens, for example. Aim to give your child a little of everything. Try different grains: offer sweet potato or butternut squash in place of standard white potatoes, and offer berries or mango instead of apples and bananas from time to time.

● keep sugar to a minimum

Sugar not only damages your baby's teeth (which can also affect his adult teeth), but also impacts on mood, immunity, sleep patterns, and weight. You don't want your child to become used to high levels of sugar and develop a "sweet tooth". If your child is over 12 months, honey can be added to foods in moderation. Children can very easily grow to love the natural sweetness of fruits and vegetables when they become used to them.

● watch out for salt

Don't add salt to your child's food. Little ones become accustomed to salty food and find healthy, unrefined foods bland without it. Children need no more than 1750mg of salt every day, and chances are they are getting more than that in their diets at present. You'll find hidden salt in foods such as bread, breakfast cereals, and even cheese. Too much salt affects children's body-water balance and can also influence the absorption of nutrients. Don't let salt creep into your child's diet.

● "good" fat versus "bad" fat

Fats, particularly EFAs (see page 9), are essential for little ones, but you want to aim for unsaturated fats, such as olive and vegetable oils, nuts, seeds, avocado, and oily fish, which are known to be beneficial to health. When eaten in excess, saturated fats, such as those found in butter, hard cheese, lard, and meat, have been linked to

tips

Keep your child hydrated. Many kids mistake thirst for hunger and can end up overeating when all they need is a drink

Think little and often. Offer smaller meals with healthy snacks in between to ensure your child gets what he needs

Avoid processed foods. These are rich in transfats, which are believed to be one of the major causes of obesity and heart disease

obesity, asthma, some cancers, and heart disease in later life, and should be offered in much smaller quantities than the unsaturated varieties. Babies and toddlers need fat, including saturated fat, but it's important to get the balance right. Avoid transfats, which are oils that have been "hydrogenated" to make them spreadable. These fats may contribute to obesity and heart disease and are used in all kinds of processed and baked food, including biscuits, crisps, and cakes.

● reducing obesity

Obesity is a concern for a growing number of parents. About 27 per cent of children above two years of age in the UK are now classified as being too heavy for their age and height, and the childhood obesity rate in the United States has almost doubled for preschool children aged 2–5 years. Learn to listen to your child. If he isn't hungry, don't push it. See pages 149–150 for tips on reducing the risk of obesity in your little one.

daily nutritional requirements

This chart sets out the amounts of vitamins and minerals recommended for children. A balanced diet, with plenty of good-quality protein, healthy fat, complex carbohydrates, and fresh vegetables and fruit will give all the vitamins and minerals your child needs.

nutrient	source	benefit	amount
vitamin A	wholegrains, nuts, seeds, meat (especially pork), corn, pulses, certain vegetables	needed for good immunity, good vision, and healthy skin	0–12 months 350mcg; 1–3 years 400mcg 30g (1oz) carrots = 380mcg
vitamin B$_1$ (thiamin)	milk and milk products, eggs, liver, green vegetables, pulses	helps with carbohydrate metabolism and normal functioning of nervous system	0–6 months 0.2mg; 7–12 months 0.3mg; 1–3 years 0.5mg 30g (1oz) lentils = 0.5mg
vitamin B$_2$ (riboflavin)	liver, lean red meat, fortified breakfast cereals, eggs	helps with energy release from food and iron transport in the body; keeps skin healthy	0–6 months 0.2mg; 7–12 months 0.4mg; 1–3 years 0.6mg 1 egg = 0.16mg
vitamin B$_3$ (niacin)	apricots, leafy green vegetables, carrots, liver, oily fish, eggs, butter, cheese, cereal, oat porridge	helps with normal functioning of nervous system, keeps body's cells healthy	0–6 months 2mg; 7–12 months 4mg; 1–3 years 6mg 30g (1oz) cereal = 5.5mg
vitamin B$_{12}$	fish, milk and milk products, meats, eggs	forms red blood cells, increases energy, improves concentration, maintains nervous system	0–6 months 0.3mcg; 7–12 months 0.4mcg; 1–3 years 0.5mcg 30g (1oz) beef = 2.1mcg
vitamin C	fresh fruit, especially berries, and vegetables, potatoes, leafy herbs	vital for healthy skin, bones, muscles, healing, and protection from viruses, allergies, and toxins; helps the body absorb iron	0–12 months 25mg; 1–3 years 30mg 30g (1oz) potatoes = 10mg
vitamin D	milk and milk products, eggs, oily fish	increases absorption of calcium from diet; essential for growth and health of bones and teeth	0–6 months 8.5mcg; 7 months to 3 years 7mcg 30g (1oz) sardines = 5.8mcg
vitamin E	nuts, seeds, eggs, milk, wholegrains, unrefined oils, leafy vegetables, avocados	needed for metabolism of essential fatty acids; protects cells of the body	0–3 years 6mg 30g (1oz) avocado = 0.6mg

● A healthy diet

Vegetables and fruit are rich in vitamins and minerals. Encourage your toddler to eat plenty by giving him manageable pieces that he can pick up with his fingers.

nutrient	source	benefit	amount
folate	leafy green vegetables, wheatgerm, pulses, liver, milk	needed for cell maintenance and repair; forms blood cells; crucial to the functioning of the nervous system	0–12 months 525mcg; 1–3 years 350mcg 30g (1oz) broccoli = 9mcg
calcium	milk and milk products, leafy green vegetables, sardines, sesame seeds, root vegetables	required for healthy bones, teeth, and muscles	0–12 months 525mg; 1–3 years 350mg 30g (1oz) hard cheese = 75mg
iron	liver, meat, poultry, dark chocolate, sardines and other fish, pulses, dark green leafy vegetables, raisins, dried apricots, fortified cereals	needed for production of haemoglobin (the oxygen-carrying part of blood) and certain enzymes; necessary for immune activity	0–3 months 1.7mg; 4–6 months 4.3mg; 7–12 months 7.8mg; 1–3 years 6.1–8.7mg 30g (1oz) poultry = 0.5mg
magnesium	brown rice, soya beans, nuts, brewer's yeast, wholegrains, milk, pulses	repairs body cells; needed for energy metabolism; maintains nerve and muscle function; keeps bones strong; promotes normal blood pressure	0–3 months 55mg; 4–6 months 60mg; 7–9 months 75mg; 10–12 months 80mg; 1–3 years 85mg 30g (1oz) brown rice = 13.2mg
potassium	bananas, potatoes, citrus fruit, dried fruit, milk and milk products	essential for muscle and heart function; helps with maintaining the baby's fluid balance	0–6 months 78–85mg; 7–12 months 70mg; 1–3 years 78mg 1 banana = 358mg
selenium	seafood and fish, poultry, meat, wholegrains, nuts, brown rice, pulses, eggs	required by the immune system; improves liver function; needed for healthy eyes, skin, and hair; protects against heart and circulatory diseases	0–6 months 6mcg; 7–12 months 10mcg; 1–3 years 15mcg 30g (1oz) white fish= 1.28mcg
zinc	seafood, poultry, lean red meats, sunflower seeds, peanuts, wholegrains, pulses	required for healthy body cells, immunity, growth, and energy metabolism	0–6 months 4mg; 7–36 months 5mg 30g (1oz) pulses = 0.39mg

food allergies

There's a lot of confusion about which foods can be given to babies. It seems that every day we hear a new story about the dangers that some foods pose to children. But what are food allergies and how common are they?

Introducing first foods to your baby should be a fun and exciting stage in your baby's development. Yet many parents regard this stage as a potential minefield, so anxious are they about allergic reaction to different foods.

The reality is that only a small proportion of people are affected by allergies. Approximately 6–8 per cent of young children and 3.7 per cent of adults in the UK and US have a food allergy. The difference between these figures is due to the fact that many children grow out of their allergies by school age.

The most common food allergies in children are to milk and eggs (the world over); peanuts (in the UK, North America, and Australia); and shellfish and fish (in South East Asia and Japan).

● when to worry

There is no need to worry unduly about food allergies unless there is a history of allergy in your family or your baby suffers from eczema. If this is not the case, it is fine to start introducing foods like meat, chicken, fish, and eggs to your baby from around six months, once you have given a variety of fruits and vegetables. I find that a lot of parents restrict their baby's diet, when in fact it's really important to give them these nutrient-rich

foods, as they need iron and essential fatty acids from six months.

However, if your family has a history of allergy (such as hayfever, asthma, eczema, or a food allergy), and particularly if your baby suffers from eczema, your baby has an increased risk of developing a food allergy. It is now no longer believed that weaning later or avoiding introducing potentially allergenic foods will affect the likelihood of developing allergies. If there is a risk of food allergy, you should try to breastfeed exclusively for six months. When weaning, introduce allergenic foods (see page 15) one at a time and wait two or three days between each to see if there is a reaction. If your child is found to be allergic to a basic food, such as cow's milk or egg, seek advice from a doctor or registered dietician on how to keep meals balanced.

● what are food allergies?

A food allergy occurs when the immune system produces allergy antibodies (known as IgE) to certain foods. These antibodies detect when the particular food has been eaten and instead of letting the body ignore it, they cause an overreaction involving the release of a chemical called histamine. Histamine causes an itchy rash,

tips

If there is no history of allergy in your family, your child is unlikely to be affected

If your child has eczema in the early stages of her life, she is at increased risk of food allergy

Berry and citrus fruits can cause redness around the mouth in kids with eczema. This is an irritant effect and rarely due to allergy

swelling and, in severe cases, difficulty in breathing. Reactions tend to occur immediately or very soon after touching or eating the food. This type of allergy is relatively well understood by doctors. Some foods, such as cow's milk, soya, wheat, and eggs, can cause delayed allergic reactions. These tend to affect babies and young children and can cause symptoms such as eczema and diarrhoea, although relatively little is known about them at present.

immediate food allergies

Immediate reactions to food occur straight after it is eaten and no more than two hours later. Reactions are often fairly mild and can include hives and facial swelling. A severe reaction can include coughing, wheezing, shortness of breath, collapse, and loss of consciousness (caused by a drop in blood pressure, known as shock). This is an anaphylactic reaction and requires urgent medical attention. Other immediate symptoms can include cramping tummy pains and vomiting.

Most immediate food allergies are due to milk, egg, peanuts, tree nuts, fish, shellfish, wheat, soya, and sesame. Allergies to milk, egg, wheat, and soya are usually outgrown, but those to peanuts, tree nuts, fish, and shellfish tend to remain for life.

nut allergy

Recent reports suggest that almost 1 in 50 UK children suffers from a nut allergy, including to peanuts. Peanut allergy is the commonest nut allergy (it seems to have doubled in a decade), and is the main cause of anaphylaxis due to food in the UK and US. The advice for parents trying to avoid nut allergies developing in their children has been the cause of some controversy. Pregnant women with a history of allergy (or with an allergic child or partner) were advised that they may wish to avoid peanuts during pregnancy and breastfeeding, as well as excluding them from their child's diet for

If your child reacts ...

✱ **Any immediate severe reaction** that includes wheezing, breathing difficulties, throat swelling, collapse, or loss of consciousness is referred to as an anaphylactic reaction. This is rare, but life-threatening. Call an ambulance immediately.

✱ **If you think your child shows signs** of a mild or delayed allergic reaction, see your GP, who can discuss this with you and can refer you to a specialist if necessary.

the first three years of their life. However, this advice has been withdrawn recently; finely ground nuts and nut butters can be offered from six months. The guidelines have changed because there is no clear evidence that avoiding nuts influences the chance of a child developing a nut allergy. Recent research indicates that including nuts in your baby's diet may even help to prevent allergy, although more research is required. If you have a family history of allergies or eczema, watch you baby carefully when introducing nuts. Never give whole nuts to children under five due to the risk of choking.

egg allergy

Egg allergies are less common than people think and children who do develop them tend to grow out of them by age six. Opinions vary, but experience has taught me that a whole egg is a perfectly healthy food for your baby from six months, provided it is fresh and cooked until solid. Children with a family history of allergy and those who suffer from eczema are more likely to have an egg allergy.

delayed food allergies

Some children have persistent, less-obvious reactions to certain foods. These delayed allergies involve a different part of the immune system that responds more slowly.

The foods most commonly involved in delayed food allergies are cow's milk and, less often, soya, wheat, and egg. The reaction to the food may take up to 48 hours to appear. Symptoms can include worsening of eczema, diarrhoea (possibly with blood and mucus), and poor weight gain. These allergies can be difficult to diagnose, as sufferers may continue to eat and drink the problem food.

Delayed food allergies are sometimes mistakenly called food intolerances. Food intolerances, however, are reactions to food, such as tummy upsets and diarrhoea, that, unlike allergies, don't involve the immune system. They tend to be more of an issue for adults than children.

diagnosing allergies

* **If you suspect an allergy**, you must see a doctor with experience in allergy. Do not attempt to diagnose it yourself.

* **The best way to diagnose an** immediate food allergy is with a skin prick test and/or a blood test. Both are used to detect the presence of antibodies called IgE, which helps to identify the problem foods. Results of these tests need to be carefully interpreted by an experienced doctor to avoid unnecessary food exclusions.

* **The most accurate way to** diagnose a delayed food allergy is to eliminate the suspected food(s) for a minimum of two weeks and see if symptoms cease. Reintroduce the foods one at a time, under the supervision of a doctor or a registered dietician, and see if the symptoms reappear. Keeping a food and symptom diary can help pinpoint which foods are the cause.

* **There are many private tests available,** such as hair analysis and kinesiology. Be careful, though, as these can be inaccurate, costly, and may put your child's health at risk.

kitchen essentials

Weaning can be daunting, but there are plenty of tools and shortcuts to make life easier. Learn how to freeze baby food safely to avoid cooking every day, and a little about food hygiene to help keep your baby healthy.

● equipment

You will probably find that you already have most of the equipment you need to make home-cooked meals, but below are a few items that will make preparing food for your child a little easier.

✳ **A mouli** or baby food grinder is good for foods that have a tough skin, like peas or dried apricots, as it produces a smooth purée, while holding back the indigestible bits.

✳ **Steamers** are great for cooking vegetables as steaming is the best way to preserve nutrients.

✳ **Electric hand blenders** are ideal for making baby purées and can handle small quantities of food.

✳ **Food processors** are good for puréeing larger quantities when making batches of purées for freezing. Many also have mini bowl attachments, which work better with smaller quantities.

✳ **A masher and bowl** is quick and easy when your baby moves on to lumpier foods.

✳ **A microwave steamer** with a valve in the lid that allows steam to be released is ideal for cooking fish or vegetables.

✳ **Freezer pots** with snap-on lids are handy and can be used as extra feeding bowls.

✳ **Ice cube trays** are great for freezing meal-sized portions of purées.

✳ **A feeding kit for babies** should include small heat-proof plastic weaning bowls, shallow soft-tipped weaning spoons, a feeding cup with a spout and two handles, and washable or wipe-clean plastic bibs.

✳ **A bouncy chair** is ideal for first meals for babies who cannot sit unaided. Once your baby can sit up, he can progress to a sturdy highchair with safety harness and wipe-clean tray.

kitchen hygiene

Food hygiene is important for everyone, but babies and young children are especially vulnerable to the effects of food poisoning, so it is essential that you take care in storing and preparing food.

Raw meat, poultry, fish, and other raw foods can easily cross-contaminate other foods. After handling these, wash your hands, utensils, and surfaces thoroughly. Use three chopping boards in different colours: one for raw, one for cooked, and one for smelly foods, such as garlic and onions. Keep raw and cooked foods apart in your fridge, with raw placed on the bottom shelf.

Using a dishwasher is generally far more hygienic than washing up by hand as it operates at a higher temperature and dries by steam rather than a tea towel, which can harbour bacteria. Only your baby's bottle and teat need to be sterilized. It's a good idea to wipe your child's highchair with an anti-bacterial surface cleaner too.

If using jars of baby food, decant the amount of food you need into a bowl and save the rest. Once a spoon with saliva has mixed with the food, you will need to use up or throw away the contents.

Don't leave perishable food out of the fridge for more than two hours and use up baby food that is stored in the fridge within 24 hours.

freezing and reheating

As your baby eats only very small quantities, especially in the early stages, it saves time to make larger batches of your baby's purée and freeze extra portions in ice cube trays or plastic freezer pots for future meals. In a couple of hours you can prepare enough food for your baby for a month.

Once food has cooled down, freeze it as soon as possible and label it with the contents and expiry date. Purées will keep for eight weeks in the freezer.

Thaw foods by defrosting them in the fridge overnight or by taking them out of the freezer several hours before a meal.

Always reheat foods until piping hot. Allow to cool and test the temperature before giving it to your baby. If reheating in a microwave, make sure that you stir the food to get rid of any uneven "hot spots". Do not reheat food more than once and never refreeze meals that have already been frozen.

helpful hints

✳ **Keep a kitchen notepad** so that you can jot down foods that you're running low on.

✳ **Keep spares of basic ingredients**, such as flour, tinned tomatoes, and vegetable oil, and when you run out of the first tin or bottle, put it on the list. Keep basics such as bread and chicken breasts in the freezer.

✳ **To extend their shelf life**, store foods such as flour, nuts, and dried fruit in sealed containers. This helps to isolate bugs too.

✳ **Save yourself time** and shop for basic ingredients online.

✳ **The temperature of your freezer** should be -18°C (0°F) and your fridge 4°C (40°F).

✳ **Make your own combinations** of purées by mixing two single ingredients together, such as a cube each of carrot and apple purée to make an apple and carrot purée.

chapter 1

feeding you both

"What you eat when you're breastfeeding is not only important for you, but for your baby too. Ahead, you'll find healthy snacks and quick, easy meals that provide the nutrients you both need, as well as advice for feeding your newborn baby."

feeding your baby

Feeding your baby isn't just about satisfying her hunger. Whether breast- or bottlefeeding, you will be spending many hours with your baby – it's a time for cuddles and for enjoying a real feeling of closeness.

Breast milk is the most natural food for your baby, so it's worth breastfeeding even for a week, as your breasts produce colostrum for the first three or four days. This thick yellow fluid is high in antibodies, which help protect your baby against infection before her immune system can start functioning properly. After two to four days, milk production is established and colostrum gradually changes into mature milk (see benefits, below).

Formula milk is made of modified cow's milk and, however hard manufacturers try, they can never mimic human breast milk – it doesn't contain the antibodies that breast milk has. However, if you are unable to breastfeed or are uncomfortable with it, you can still give your baby a good start with formula milk. See page 24 for advice.

● beginning breastfeeding

Feeds can take anything from 10 to 40 minutes, so find a comfortable, calm place to breastfeed. The more relaxed you are, the better it will be for your baby. Choose a chair with arms, which

benefits of breast milk

Why is it so important to breastfeed my baby?

Breast milk is packed with antibodies and strengthens babies' immune systems, which is particularly important for premature babies. It is rich in omega-3 essential fatty acids, which are important for brain development, and contains prebiotics that help with the development of gut immunity.

It is believed that breastfeeding for just one month has health benefits for the first 14 years of your child's life. Research has shown it protects babies from ear, chest, and gastrointestinal infections, asthma, childhood diabetes, eczema, and even obesity. The composition of breast milk changes to meet all your baby's needs; firstly quenching her thirst and then providing her with calories and nutrients.

ask annabel

supports your back (you may need a cushion). Keep a glass of water nearby, as breastfeeding can make you feel thirsty. Your feet should reach the floor so that your knees and lap are level. Bring your baby to your breast, rather than leaning over.

technique

It is important that your baby opens her mouth wide and takes the nipple and a good proportion of the areola surrounding it into her mouth in order to stimulate your breast to produce milk. If your baby sucks just on your nipple, she will get frustrated as she won't be able to get enough milk, and you may get sore, cracked nipples.

If it feels very uncomfortable, gently insert your little finger in your baby's mouth between your breast and the corner of her mouth and start again.

one breast or two?

The milk you produce changes during a feed. The early part consists of foremilk, which is thin and white and is a thirst-quenching drink that is high in lactose (sugar), but low in fat. The latter part of the feed consists of hindmilk, which is thicker, creamier in colour, and contains two to three times the fat, and one and a half times the protein.

It is important to make sure your baby has completely emptied the first breast (including the hindmilk) before putting her on the second. It is the small amount of hindmilk at the end of the feed that will help your baby go longer between feeds. Some babies need about 30 minutes to empty the breast. If you gently squeeze your nipple between your thumb and forefinger you will be able to check if there is any milk left in the breast.

establishing a good milk supply

Let your baby decide when she needs to feed and when she has had enough. All breastfeeding counsellors agree that in order to produce enough milk, it is essential that the breasts are stimulated frequently during the first few weeks and that the mother maintains a good fluid and food intake.

To begin with, your baby will take very small amounts as her stomach is only about the size of a walnut, but if she is allowed to feed as often as she wants she will be letting your breasts know how much milk she needs. The more often she feeds and the more milk she takes, the more you will supply. This is known as supply and demand.

breastfeeding essentials

* **Nursing bras** These need to be firm enough to prevent your breasts from sagging, but not too tight. They should be cotton with wide straps and a front opening, allowing you to undo one side at a time using one hand.

* **Breast pads** You can buy disposable breast pads to absorb leaks. Don't leave soggy breast pads for a prolonged period as it can contribute to soreness and infection.

* **Nursing pillow** A horseshoe or V-shaped cushion is ideal for supporting your baby in a comfortable breastfeeding position.

* **Breast pump** A manual or electric pump may be easier than hand expressing. Store the milk in sterile containers in the fridge for up to 24 hours or freeze it.

tips

Milk creates an ideal breeding ground for bacteria, so it's vital to keep bottles and teats scrupulously clean and to sterilize them

Do not use softened water to make up your baby's formula milk, as it is high in salt, which is harmful for your baby's kidneys

Do not give soya formula to babies under six months. It should only be given under the advice of a dietician or paediatrician

Some women adjust to breastfeeding easily, but many find it hard. If you are feeling frustrated, remember that you are not alone. Call a breastfeeding counsellor, your midwife, or health visitor for advice. It's worth persevering.

establishing a routine

At first you will find that your baby feeds very frequently and it is difficult to predict when your baby will sleep.

As time goes on, your baby's feeds will become more predictable and she will be able to go for longer stretches between feeds. Once your milk supply is established at around six weeks, you can start trying to get your baby into a routine. Feeding every three hours or so is an average timespan, but babies have growth spurts when they may want to feed more often, and also times when they need to sleep more, so a routine should be fairly flexible. Record your baby's feeds on page 25.

combining breast and bottle

Many mothers do manage to successfully combine breast and bottle, and this may suit women who return to work. Once breastfeeding is fully established at around six weeks, you can introduce the occasional bottle of formula milk so

that your baby doesn't reject the bottle when you wean her. For some mothers, however, giving formula can impact on their supply of breast milk.

You can of course express milk at work if there is a quiet, private place to do it. You will also need access to a fridge, and a cool bag and ice packs to keep the milk cold until you travel home. Expressed milk keeps for four hours at room temperature and eight days in the coldest part of the fridge, and up to three months in the freezer. Store in a sterilized sealed container, marked with the date on which it was expressed.

refusing a bottle

Sometimes breastfed babies will refuse to take a bottle. This can be very difficult, especially if you are going back to work. Here are some tips:

* **Get someone else to offer the bottle**, so your baby doesn't smell your breast milk.
* **Offer the bottle** when you are face-to-face with your baby, perhaps while she is in a bouncy chair – that way she doesn't expect to be breastfed.
* **Experiment with different teats** or soften the teat in boiling water, allowing it to cool down.
* **By six months** many babies are able to drink from a cup, so you may be able to avoid giving her bottles altogether.

● bottlefeeding

If you prefer to bottlefeed you will need to give your baby infant formula milk up until the age of one year. Ordinary cow's milk is unsuitable before then as it does not contain enough iron or nutrients for proper growth. Many women choose to give their babies formula milk and there are advantages:

✳ **You can see exactly how much milk** your baby is getting at each feed.

✳ **Formula milk takes longer to digest** than breast milk, so babies tend to go longer between feeds.

✳ **Your partner can share** in the pleasure of feeding – giving you more freedom and a better night's sleep.

● position for bottlefeeding

✳ **Hold your baby close to you** on your lap in a semi-upright position, where she can make eye contact with you. She will enjoy feeding more if you smile and chat to her.

✳ **Make sure you tilt the bottle** so that the neck and teat are full of milk to avoid pockets of air, which could cause your baby to have wind.

✳ **If your baby seems unsettled** during the feed, she may have wind. Sit her up and try to get her to burp by rubbing her back.

● making up formula milk

It is best to make up your baby's milk just before a feed to avoid risk of contamination from bacteria. When out and about, it's easiest to fill sterilized bottles with water and measure out the right number of scoops of formula into separate lidded containers. When you're ready to feed, warm the water, add the formula, and shake them together.

dealing with reflux

✳ **If your baby** continually brings up her feeds, seems to be in pain during feeding, is only taking small amounts of milk, and cries excessively, it is possible that she has reflux.

✳ **Reflux is when a weak valve** at the top of a baby's stomach allows the feed, along with gastric juices, to come back up, causing vomiting and a burning sensation. Consult your GP for a diagnosis.

✳ **If your baby has reflux**, hold her in an upright position during and for about 20 minutes after each feed. Try giving her smaller, more frequent feeds too. Raising the head of her cot a little off the ground may also help. In more severe cases a pre-thickened formula milk or antacid may help.

✳ **Reflux almost always** gets better in time – starting solids is often the turning point.

● how much milk?

To begin with, your baby needs to feed little and often and may need to feed every two hours. The amount of fluid a baby needs is generally calculated according to her weight. From birth, babies below 5kg (11lb) need 120–150ml (4–5fl oz) of formula milk per kg (2¼lb) of their weight over a 24 hour period. For example, if your baby weighs 3kg (6½lb), give her 450ml (16fl oz) of formula milk a day. Older babies who are 5–10kg (11–22lb) need a minimum of 500–600ml (17–21fl oz) of formula milk a day and water can be introduced too. Give your baby milk as often as she requires it.

baby's feeding routine

Use this space to record your baby's milk feeds as you settle her into a routine. Feeding every three hours is an average routine, but this is dependent on many factors, such as growth spurts and whether it's breast or formula milk. Flexibility is key!

feeding you

Your diet is just as important when you're breastfeeding as it was when you were pregnant because you are the primary source of nourishment for your baby. A good diet will also help you to cope with the demands of a new baby.

Keeping up a good milk supply is not only dependent on you eating and drinking well, you also need to look after yourself and take some rest, especially if your baby is keeping you up at night.

● what to eat

Breastfeeding is one of the best ways for you to regain your prenatal figure – it burns on average about 500 calories a day – the equivalent of running 6.5–8km (4–5 miles). Although you are no doubt keen to lose the extra weight as soon as possible, you shouldn't embark on a crash diet when breastfeeding. Instead, avoid "empty" calories and eat a healthy diet with plenty of fresh fruit, vegetables, lean meats, fish, and wholegrains. It is important to eat a variety of foods, including:

✳ Fruit and vegetables, especially those rich in vitamin C such as kiwi fruit, strawberries, and broccoli, as these help boost iron absorption.

✳ Protein-rich foods such as lean meat, chicken, fish, eggs, and pulses.

✳ Red meat, which is great for new mothers as it is rich in iron.

✳ Oily fish, like salmon, fresh tuna or sardines, should be consumed twice a week.

✳ Starchy food, such as bread, pasta and rice. Wholegrain varieties are especially good and help

prevent bowel problems such as constipation (which many women experience after childbirth).

✳ Dairy products – milk, cheese, and yogurt are important as they are rich in calcium. Other calcium-rich foods include dark green leafy vegetables, sesame seeds, and tinned sardines. Your body adapts to your baby's needs during breastfeeding and may provide enough calcium for you both, but it's recommended that you increase your calcium intake.

✳ Healthy snacks are key because you often want smaller meals when breastfeeding. It's worth preparing some tasty snacks that you can dip into during the day. Try my Honey and soy toasted seeds (page 29) or make up a bowl of chicken or salmon pasta salad (see pages 46–47 for salad recipes) and store it in the fridge. You can also buy easy-to-prepare, healthy snacks such as raw vegetables and pita bread with hummus.

● taking care

Eating fish is good for your health and the development of your baby. It's fine to eat as much white fish as you like. Oily fish is particularly beneficial for the development of your baby's brain and vision, so try to include two portions a week of oily fish in your diet. However, don't eat more than

tips

Eat plenty of iron-rich foods, such as red meat, leafy green vegetables, and pulses as you may lack iron after childbirth

Have healthy snacks to hand as you'll probably want to eat smaller meals while breastfeeding

Fluids are essential for breastfeeding mums. Aim to drink 8–12 glasses of water a day

"Breastfeeding is one of the best ways for you to regain your prenatal figure – it burns on average about 500 calories a day"

two portions as these fish contain tiny amounts of pollutants, some of which can be passed into your breast milk. You should avoid eating more than one portion a week of shark, swordfish and marlin because these predator fish have high levels of mercury. Tinned tuna isn't classed as an oily fish

because canning reduces the fat (containing the pollutants), so it is fine to have up to four regular tins of tuna a week.

I've already talked about allergies on pages 14–16, but I thought I'd reiterate this here. Women with a history of food allergy (or with an allergic partner or child) were advised that they may wish to avoid peanuts during breastfeeding. However, this advice has recently been withdrawn by the Department of Health as there is no evidence to suggest that a mother's diet during breastfeeding influences the development of food allergy. Recent

benefits for you

I know that breastfeeding is great for my baby, but is it true that it has additional benefits for me?

Breastfeeding helps you to lose your baby weight as it uses up at least 500 calories a day (approximately the number of calories in a large shop-bought muffin, a bacon sandwich, or a 100g/3½oz chocolate bar). You can eat more than usual and still shed your pregnancy weight. Also, a baby sucking at the breast causes the uterus to contract, which helps it to return to its normal size much faster. Research also suggests that breastfeeding helps protect mothers from ovarian cancer, breast cancer, and osteoporosis (brittle bones). Holding your baby close while breastfeeding is also a great way to bond with your little one.

ask annabel

studies suggest that peanut allergies may actually be prevented if children are exposed to peanuts during weaning. Feeding your baby a variety of foods between 6 and 12 months is thought to help prevent allergies developing in later life. Research also indicates that exclusive breastfeeding for six months may help to prevent allergies in susceptible babies.

Some people believe that eating certain foods, such as cauliflower, broccoli or onions, can affect breast milk and cause colic, and some mums swear that hot and spicy foods upset their baby. In my experience, I have found that the majority of babies are not sensitive to what you are eating and there's no firm evidence for this, so unless you notice that your baby regularly has a reaction to certain foods in your diet, I wouldn't worry unduly. The best advice is to follow a well-balanced diet with a little bit of what you fancy.

● what to drink

Drinking plenty of fluids is essential for breastfeeding mums. You should drink between 2.5 and 3 litres (4½ –5 pints) a day, or about 8 to 12 glasses. Try to space this out during the day. This can be tap or bottled water but it doesn't all have to be water. Drinking some fruit juice is fine; choose pure fruit juice with no added sugar.

You can have tea or coffee, but try to limit caffeinated drinks to two cups a day, as caffeine can pass from your blood into your breast milk. If your baby becomes agitated or finds it difficult to settle when you have been drinking caffeinated drinks, you may want to avoid them or switch to a decaffeinated alternative. Try herbal teas like chamomile or peppermint tea, which can also help to calm and destress you if you are having a tough day.

Alcohol, like caffeine, passes from your blood into your breast milk. If you want to drink alcohol, do so when you know you will not have to breastfeed for at least two or three hours, and don't have more than one or two drinks a day.

● vitamin supplements

It is your body rather than your milk supply that will suffer if you aren't eating a good diet. The nutrients in your diet are passed on to your baby through your breast milk. Only the surplus is used to nourish your body, so it's a good idea to take a postnatal vitamin supplement. Your iron stores may be low after giving birth and you'll have an increased need for vitamin D during breastfeeding, so choose a daily multivitamin supplement with 10mcg of vitamin D and 10mg of iron.

swiss muesli

This is based on the delicious muesli that they serve for breakfast at The Wolseley, in London. It should help to keep your energy levels up all morning. If you prefer, you can leave out the extra milk and add a small grated apple instead.

- PREPARATION: 10 MINUTES, PLUS AT LEAST 1 HOUR SOAKING
- COOKING: NONE
- MAKES 1 PORTION
- PROVIDES PROTEIN, FIBRE, IRON, VITS B_1, B_2, B_3, C, D, & E

30g (1oz) rolled oats

8–9 tbsp milk

1 tbsp double cream

1 tbsp sultanas

1 tbsp raisins

1 tbsp dried cranberries

3 ready-to-eat dried apricots, chopped

4–5 hazelnuts, finely chopped

1 tsp sunflower seeds

4–5 shelled unsalted pistachios, chopped

Small handful of fresh berries (e.g. blueberries or raspberries), to serve

1 tsp clear honey, to serve

Put the oats in a bowl with 6 tbsp milk and leave to soak in the fridge for 1 hour, or overnight. Before serving, stir in the cream, dried fruit, hazelnuts, seeds, and the remaining 2–3 tbsp milk (add a little more milk, if you like). Sprinkle over the pistachios. Serve with fresh berries, drizzled with a little honey.

honey and soy toasted seeds

Pack this tasty and nutritious snack in individual portion bags.

- PREPARATION: 2–3 MINUTES, PLUS COOLING
- COOKING: 3 MINUTES
- MAKES 150G (5½OZ)
- PROVIDES FIBRE, OMEGA-3s, VITS A & E

1 tbsp sunflower oil

75g (2½oz) pumpkin seeds

75g (2½oz) sunflower seeds

1 tbsp honey

1 tbsp soy sauce

Heat the sunflower oil in a non-stick frying pan, add the pumpkin and sunflower seeds, and cook, stirring constantly, for about 2 minutes until the seeds are lightly browned. Remove from the heat and stir in the honey and soy sauce. Return to the heat for 1 minute. Spread out on a non-stick baking tray and leave to cool. When cold, store in an airtight container.

notes

notes..

granola bars

Flax seeds (also called linseed) are extremely rich in omega-3 oils, similar to the type found in salmon and other oily fish. Wheatgerm contains a lot of folate and vitamin E. They both have a slightly nutty taste, which helps to make these oat bars extra delicious.

- PREPARATION: 15 MINUTES
- COOKING: ABOUT 30 MINUTES
- MAKES 8 BARS
- PROVIDES FIBRE, OMEGA-3s, IRON, FOLATE, VITS A & E, PREBIOTICS

110g (4oz) rolled oats

45g (1½oz) sunflower seeds

55g (2oz) pecan nuts, roughly chopped

30g (1oz) wheatgerm

55g (2oz) raisins

55g (2oz) dried cranberries

30g (1oz) flax seeds

170g (6oz) golden syrup or clear honey

55g (2oz) soft light brown sugar

55g (2oz) butter, plus extra for greasing

1 tsp pure vanilla extract

½ tsp salt

Preheat the oven to 150°C (130°C fan), gas 2. Lightly grease a 28 x 19cm (11 x 7½in) cake tin with butter, and line the bottom and sides of the tin with baking parchment. Set aside.

Mix the oats, sunflower seeds, pecans, wheatgerm, raisins, cranberries, and flax seeds together in a large bowl. Put the syrup, sugar, and butter in a saucepan and warm gently until the butter has melted and the sugar has dissolved. Remove from the heat and stir in the vanilla extract and salt, then pour over the oat mixture. Stir with a wooden spoon until everything is well combined. Press firmly into the cake tin (a potato masher is good for this).

Bake for 30 minutes until the centre is just firm (if using honey you may need to bake for an extra 5 minutes). Remove from the oven and allow to cool for 15 minutes, then mark into bars with a sharp knife. Leave to cool completely before removing the bars from the tin. Store in the refrigerator.

baked cod gratin

This dish uses a very simple cheese sauce that can easily be made while the fish is cooking. However, you can substitute a good-quality ready-made cheese sauce, if you prefer.

- PREPARATION: 15 MINUTES
- COOKING: ABOUT 15 MINUTES
- MAKES 2 PORTIONS
- PROVIDES PROTEIN, CALCIUM, IRON, SELENIUM, VITS A & D

250g (9oz) baby leaf spinach, carefully washed

Salt and pepper

15g (½oz) butter

2 x 140g (5oz) pieces of skinless cod fillet, about 1cm (½in) thick

1 heaped tbsp cornflour

150ml (5fl oz) milk

30g (1oz) Gruyère or mature Cheddar cheese, grated

3 tbsp freshly grated Parmesan cheese

1 egg yolk

¼ tsp Dijon mustard

Pinch of paprika or cayenne pepper

Preheat the oven to 220°C (200°C fan), gas 7. Preheat the grill to high.

Heat 2 tbsp water in a large saucepan over a high heat. When it is steaming pack the spinach into the pan and cover tightly with a lid. Cook for 2–3 minutes, stirring halfway through, until the spinach has wilted. Transfer the spinach to a colander and squeeze out as much water as possible by pressing the spinach against the colander with a wooden spoon. Season to taste with salt and pepper.

Lightly butter a small ovenproof dish using half of the butter. Arrange the cooked spinach in the bottom of the dish. Season the cod with a little salt and pepper and sit the fillets on the spinach. Dot with the remaining butter. Bake for 10 minutes until the fish is just opaque all the way through. (Thicker fillets may take a couple of minutes longer.)

Meanwhile, mix the cornflour with 2 tbsp of the milk to a paste, then add to the remaining milk in a saucepan. Gently bring to the boil, whisking for about 4 minutes until thickened. Mix the Gruyère and 1 tbsp Parmesan into the hot sauce until the cheese has melted. Stir in the egg yolk and mustard, then season to taste with salt, pepper, and paprika or cayenne.

Remove the dish from the oven. Spoon the sauce over the fish and spinach, then sprinkle over the remaining Parmesan. Grill for 2–3 minutes until the sauce is lightly browned and bubbling.

notes

notes...

sweet root soup

Soups can make a satisfying lunch or snack and are useful to have in the fridge to heat up quickly if you feel hungry. Carrots, sweet potatoes, and squash all have high levels of beta-carotene, a powerful antioxidant. I quite like fairly thick soups, but if you prefer a thinner consistency, you can add a little more stock after the soup has been blended.

- PREPARATION: 15–20 MINUTES
- COOKING: 30–45 MINUTES
- MAKES 4 PORTIONS
- PROVIDES BETA-CAROTENE, FOLATE, VITS C & E
- SUITABLE FOR FREEZING

1 tbsp olive oil

1 medium red onion, chopped

2 carrots, peeled and diced

1 small sweet potato, peeled and diced (250g/9oz)

½ small butternut squash, peeled and diced (150g/5½oz peeled weight)

1 tsp mild curry paste

1 tsp clear honey

600ml (1 pint) vegetable stock

Salt and pepper

Crème fraîche, to serve (optional)

Fresh coriander leaves, to garnish (optional)

Heat the oil in a large pan and sauté the vegetables for 10–15 minutes until turning soft. Stir in the curry paste and honey, and cook for 1 minute. Add the stock and bring up to a simmer, then cook uncovered for 20–25 minutes until the vegetables are tender.

Allow to cool slightly before blending until smooth (be careful when blending hot liquids). Season to taste. Warm gently before serving. This is particularly nice if you top each bowl of soup with a small spoonful of crème fraîche and a few coriander leaves.

> "Carrots are one of nature's top sources of vitamin C, and, interestingly, cooked carrots have twice the antioxidant power of raw carrots"

bag-baked salmon

Oily fish such as salmon contains plenty of omega-3 fatty acids, which are good for both you and your baby. These bags can be assembled earlier in the day and then kept in the refrigerator until needed.

- PREPARATION: 10–15 MINUTES
- COOKING: ABOUT 15 MINUTES
- MAKES 2 PORTIONS
- PROVIDES PROTEIN, OMEGA-3s, IRON, SELENIUM, BETA-CAROTENE, VIT E

¼ red pepper, thinly sliced

2 fresh shiitake or oyster mushrooms, stalks removed and thinly sliced

2 x 170g (6oz) pieces of salmon fillet, about 2.5cm (1in) thick

2 large spring onions, thinly sliced

½ tsp grated fresh root ginger

2 tsp soy sauce

1 tbsp mirin

½ tsp caster sugar

Preheat the oven to 200°C (180°C fan), gas 6. Cut out two rectangles of foil about 40 x 30cm (16 x 12in), and two of baking parchment the same size.

Lay the foil rectangles on a flat surface and put a piece of baking parchment on top of each. Mix the red pepper and mushrooms together and spoon half into the centre of each piece of parchment. Sit the salmon on top of the vegetables and scatter on the spring onions. Mix together the ginger, soy sauce, mirin, and sugar until the sugar has dissolved, then carefully spoon over the salmon.

Bring the long sides of the foil and parchment together over the salmon and roll and fold over to seal. Twist and scrunch the ends together so that the salmon is completely enclosed. Set the bags on a baking tray and bake for about 15 minutes until the salmon is opaque all the way through and flakes when pressed with a fork. Undo the parcels and transfer the salmon to a plate, then spoon over the vegetables and sauce.

> Oily fish is the best source of essential fatty acids. Juices, yogurts, and cereal bars are often enriched with omega-3s, but these are mostly plant-derived, and are less beneficial

notes

sandwiches and wraps

If you are out and about during the day, or going to work, why not prepare a sandwich or wrap in the morning and take it with you? They make fast and satisfying lunches or snacks, especially if you pack them full of crisp salad and lean meats. Adding a tasty dressing means that they won't let you down on flavour either. Here are a few of my favourite sandwich and wrap ideas.

turkey and tomato sandwich with honey-mustard mayo

I like wild rocket, which has a peppery bite, but if you are not keen on this then use baby spinach leaves instead. This also makes a nice filling for a flour tortilla wrap.

- PREPARATION: 5 MINUTES
- COOKING: NONE
- MAKES 1 PORTION
- PROVIDES PROTEIN, FIBRE, IRON, ZINC, SELENIUM, VITS A, B_1, B_2, C, & E

2 tbsp mayonnaise (reduced fat is fine)

1 tsp wholegrain mustard (or to taste)

½ tsp clear honey

2 slices wholegrain bread

2 thin slices cooked turkey breast (about 55g/2oz)

1 medium tomato, thinly sliced

Handful of wild rocket

Salt and pepper

Mix the mayonnaise, mustard, and honey together and spread half over one side of one of the slices of bread. Lay the turkey on top, followed by the tomato and rocket. Season to taste with salt and pepper. Spread the remaining mayonnaise over the second slice of bread and press down on the rocket. Cut the sandwich in half to serve.

“ Turkey contains more zinc than chicken, and zinc helps to boost the immune system. It also contains tryptophan, which the body uses to make the "happy" chemical serotonin ”

chicken and avocado wrap

This is also good as a sandwich made with multigrain bread.

- PREPARATION: 5 MINUTES
- COOKING: NONE
- MAKES 1 PORTION
- PROVIDES PROTEIN, FIBRE, IRON, ZINC, SELENIUM, VITS A & E

1½ tbsp mayonnaise (reduced fat is fine)

2 tsp lemon juice

1 flour tortilla wrap

Small handful of cress or alfalfa

2 thin slices cooked chicken breast (about 55g/2oz)

½ small (Hass) avocado, thinly sliced

Salt and pepper

Mix the mayonnaise and lemon juice together in a small bowl. Warm the tortilla in the microwave for 5–10 seconds until soft, then spread over the lemon mayonnaise. Scatter the cress down the centre and lay the chicken on top, followed by the avocado. Season with a little salt and pepper, then roll up the wrap and cut in half. Secure each half with a cocktail stick.

chinese-style beef wrap

This wrap reminds me of one of my favourite Chinese dishes – duck pancakes. Beansprouts and lettuce make a super-quick filling, but if you have extra time replace them with a thinly sliced spring onion and a handful of matchstick-sized strips of cucumber.

- PREPARATION: 5 MINUTES
- COOKING: NONE
- MAKES 1 PORTION
- PROVIDES PROTEIN, FIBRE, IRON, ZINC, SELENIUM, VITS C & E

1 tbsp mayonnaise (reduced fat is fine)

2 tsp plum sauce

Large squeeze of lemon juice

1 flour tortilla wrap

2 thin slices roast beef (about 55g/2oz), or cooked chicken

15g (½oz) beansprouts

15g (½oz) shredded lettuce

Salt and pepper

Mix together the mayonnaise, plum sauce, and lemon juice. Warm the tortilla in the microwave for 10 seconds, then spread over the mayonnaise mixture. Lay the beef (or chicken) down the centre and scatter the beansprouts and lettuce on top. Season with a little salt and pepper, then roll up and cut in half. Secure each half with a cocktail stick.

notes

sesame beef and broccoli stir-fry

You can prepare all the ingredients for this stir-fry in advance and keep them, covered, in the fridge until ready to cook. It will then take only a few minutes to have supper on the table.

- PREPARATION: 10 MINUTES
- COOKING: 15 MINUTES
- MAKES 2 PORTIONS
- PROVIDES PROTEIN, IRON, SELENIUM, ZINC, CALCIUM, FOLATE, VITS A & B$_{12}$

110g (4oz) medium egg noodles

1 tbsp plus 1 tsp sunflower oil

1 tsp toasted sesame oil

1 tbsp sesame seeds

½ red chilli, deseeded and thinly sliced (optional)

1 clove garlic, crushed

½ tsp grated fresh root ginger

140g (5oz) broccoli, broken into small florets

225g (8oz) beef sirloin or fillet steak, cut into small strips

2 large spring onions, thinly sliced

4 tbsp oyster sauce

1 tsp caster sugar

1½ tbsp soy sauce (or to taste)

Cook the noodles according to the packet instructions. Drain and rinse with cold water, then toss with 1 tsp sunflower oil and the sesame oil. Set aside.

Put the sesame seeds in a wok set over a medium heat and toast for 1–2 minutes. Transfer to a bowl and set aside. Add the remaining sunflower oil to the wok together with the chilli (if using), garlic, and ginger. Cook for a minute, then add the broccoli and beef, and stir-fry for 6 minutes until the broccoli is tender and the beef is cooked.

Add the noodles, spring onions, oyster sauce, sugar, and soy sauce, and cook for 2 minutes. Sprinkle over the sesame seeds before serving.

" Many young mums are deficient in iron, which leaves them feeling tired. Red meat provides the best source of iron, helping to boost energy and concentration "

seared tuna with coriander couscous

Tuna and other oily fish are the best sources of omega-3 essential fatty acids, which are very important for the development of a baby's eyesight and brain (a baby's brain triples in size in the first year). It is thought that omega-3s can pass to your baby through your breast milk. So try to eat two portions of oily fish a week.

- PREPARATION: 10 MINUTES, PLUS 1 HOUR MARINATING
- COOKING: 5 MINUTES, PLUS 5 MINUTES STANDING
- MAKES 2 PORTIONS
- PROVIDES PROTEIN, OMEGA-3s, IRON, SELENIUM, VITS B_1, B_3, & C

2 tbsp soy sauce

2 tbsp mirin

1 tbsp soft light brown sugar

1 x 225g (8oz) fresh tuna steak, about 1.5cm (5⁄8in) thick

1 tbsp sunflower oil

Couscous

125g (4½oz) couscous

1 tbsp olive oil

200ml (7fl oz) hot vegetable stock

2 spring onions, thinly sliced

Handful of fresh coriander leaves, roughly chopped

1 tbsp lime juice (or to taste)

Salt and pepper

Mix the soy sauce, mirin, and sugar together in a large dish. Add the tuna and turn to coat. Leave to marinate in the fridge for 1 hour, turning the tuna over halfway through. (Don't marinate longer or the tuna will turn mushy.)

Meanwhile, put the couscous in a large bowl and stir in the olive oil, followed by the hot stock. Cover the bowl tightly with cling film and leave to stand for 5 minutes until the stock has been absorbed. Uncover and fluff up the couscous with a fork, then gently stir in the spring onions, coriander, and lime juice. Season with salt and pepper. Spread out on two plates.

Put a ridged grill pan over a high heat and brush with sunflower oil. Remove the tuna from the marinade (reserve the marinade) and pat dry with kitchen paper. Sear on the hot grill pan for 2 minutes on each side for medium-cooked tuna (thinner pieces of tuna will cook more quickly). Rest the tuna on a plate for 5 minutes.

Put the reserved marinade in a small saucepan with 2 tbsp water. Bring up to the boil and bubble for 1 minute, to make a sauce. Slice the tuna and lay it on the couscous, then drizzle over the sauce.

pasta with rocket and mascarpone sauce

This sauce is so quick that you can make it while the pasta is cooking. If you like garlic then add a small clove to the food processor with the rocket. You can also toss in a handful of cherry tomatoes (halved) at the end for a bit of bright colour contrast.

- PREPARATION: 10 MINUTES
- COOKING: 8–10 MINUTES
- MAKES 2 PORTIONS
- PROVIDES PROTEIN, CALCIUM, FOLATE, VITS A, C, D, & E

225g (8oz) pasta bows, spirals, or corkscrews

110g (4oz) wild rocket (4 handfuls)

125g (4½oz) mascarpone (half of a 250g tub)

4 tbsp freshly grated Parmesan cheese, plus extra to serve

2 tsp lemon juice

Salt and pepper

Cook the pasta according to the packet instructions. Meanwhile, put the rocket in the bowl of a food processor and whiz until finely chopped. Add the mascarpone, Parmesan, and lemon juice, and whiz again to combine (if the mascarpone is very thick and creamy, you might need to add 1 tbsp milk). Season to taste with salt and pepper.

Drain the pasta well and return to the pan. Add the rocket sauce and toss to coat the pasta. Serve with extra Parmesan.

notes

frittata provençale

I may be mixing my countries a bit in the title here, but a flat omelette bolstered with summer vegetables makes a lovely quick lunch or light supper. This is also good cold, so keep leftovers in the fridge for a time when you need a quick snack.

- PREPARATION: 20 MINUTES
- COOKING: 25 MINUTES
- MAKES 4–6 PORTIONS
- PROVIDES PROTEIN, BETA-CAROTENE, FOLATE, VITS C, D, & E, PREBIOTICS

3–4 new potatoes

6 eggs

1 tsp chopped fresh thyme leaves (or other herbs such as chives, parsley, tarragon, and chervil)

4 tbsp crème fraîche or double cream

Salt and pepper

2 tbsp olive oil

1 small red onion, thinly sliced

½ red pepper, thinly sliced

1 medium courgette, thinly sliced

1 clove garlic, crushed

110g (4oz) Gruyère cheese, grated

2 tbsp freshly grated Parmesan cheese

Cook the potatoes in boiling salted water for about 12 minutes until just tender. When cool enough to handle, cut into slices and set aside. Beat the eggs in a jug with the thyme and crème fraîche. Season well with salt and pepper and set aside.

Heat the oil in a medium non-stick frying pan (20–23cm/8–9in) and sauté the onion, red pepper, and courgette for 8–10 minutes until just soft. Add the garlic and potatoes, and cook for a further minute. Spread out the vegetables in the pan, then pour in the eggs. Cook for 2–3 minutes, stirring occasionally. Leave to cook for a further 6–7 minutes until the frittata is just set underneath, but still wobbly on top. Meanwhile, preheat the grill to high.

Scatter the cheeses over the frittata and grill for 2–4 minutes until the cheese is golden brown and bubbly and the frittata has set on top. Remove from the grill and leave to stand for 5 minutes.

Loosen the frittata from the pan using a spatula, then slide out on to a large plate. Cut into wedges to serve.

> Buy omega-3-enriched eggs, laid by hens that are fed oil-rich seeds. Research shows that these may be good for babies' brain and eye development

notes

notes ....

southwestern salad

Sweetcorn and beans contain complementary amino acids, which means that when they are combined they are a great source of protein. Corn is also rich in folate. Crunchy salads tossed in tangy dressings are popular in southern California and the southwestern states of the USA.

● PREPARATION: 10 MINUTES

● COOKING: NONE

● MAKES 2 PORTIONS

● PROVIDES PROTEIN, FIBRE, CALCIUM, IRON, BETA-CAROTENE, VITS B_2, C, & E

2 tbsp mayonnaise (reduced fat is fine)

2 tbsp natural yogurt

1 tsp lemon juice

1–2 tbsp milk

2 tsp chopped fresh dill or coriander

Salt and pepper

1 x 198g tin sweetcorn, drained

½ x 410g tin kidney beans, drained and rinsed

½ red pepper, diced

2 spring onions, thinly sliced

¼ iceberg or ½ romaine lettuce

1 avocado, sliced

In a large bowl whisk together the mayonnaise, yogurt, and lemon juice. Whisk in enough milk to give a coating consistency, then stir in the dill and season with salt and pepper. Add the sweetcorn, beans, red pepper, and spring onions, and toss to coat in the dressing. Cover and chill until needed.

Just before serving, put the lettuce in the bottom of a salad bowl and spoon the tossed salad on top, then scatter over the avocado slices.

chicken, broccoli, and mangetout pasta salad

Broccoli is king of the Superfood vegetables, being rich in a wide range of nutrients. It also helps to strengthen the immune system and is a major force in fighting various forms of cancer.

- PREPARATION: 10 MINUTES
- COOKING: 10 MINUTES
- MAKES 2 PORTIONS
- PROVIDES PROTEIN, OMEGA-3s, IRON, ZINC, SELENIUM, FOLATE, VITS A & C

110g (4oz) pasta spirals

55g (2oz) small broccoli florets

30g (1oz) mangetout

3 tbsp sunflower oil

½ tsp toasted sesame oil

2 tsp rice wine vinegar

2 tsp clear honey

2 tsp soy sauce

110g (4oz) cooked chicken, thinly sliced

30g (1oz) pumpkin seeds

Cook the pasta according to packet instructions, adding the broccoli and mangetout 2 minutes before the end of the cooking time. Drain and immediately rinse well with cold water. Drain well again.

Whisk together the oils, vinegar, honey, and soy sauce in a large bowl. Add the pasta and vegetables and toss to coat, then cover and refrigerate until needed. Just before serving, add the chicken and toss again, then sprinkle over the pumpkin seeds.

salmon, cucumber, and dill pasta salad

A well-balanced meal should contain a combination of proteins and carbohydrate, to enable the body to repair and refuel. This salad contains both and the pasta is fairly low on the glycaemic index, which means that it breaks down slowly and helps to keep energy levels steady. Salmon takes only a few minutes to cook in the microwave, so this is quick and easy to prepare.

- PREPARATION: 10 MINUTES
- COOKING: 10–12 MINUTES
- MAKES 2 PORTIONS
- PROVIDES PROTEIN, OMEGA-3s, IRON, SELENIUM, VITS A, C, & E

110g (4oz) pasta bows
75g (2½oz) cucumber

2 tbsp crème fraîche (half fat is fine)

1 tbsp mayonnaise (reduced fat is fine)

2–3 tsp lemon juice (to taste)

2 tsp chopped fresh dill

2 spring onions, thinly sliced

Salt and pepper

150g (5½oz) salmon fillet, cooked (see below), skinned, and flaked

Cook the pasta according to the packet instructions. Drain and rinse with cold water, then drain again well. While the pasta is cooking, peel the cucumber, cut in half lengthways, and scoop out the seeds with a teaspoon. Slice the cucumber thinly.

Mix the crème fraîche, mayonnaise, lemon juice, and dill together in a large bowl. Add the pasta, cucumber, and spring onions. Toss well and season to taste with salt and pepper. Cover and refrigerate until needed. Just before serving, scatter over the flaked salmon.

Note: To cook the salmon in the microwave, put it in a fairly deep glass dish and season with a little salt and pepper. Add 3 tbsp water plus a squeeze of lemon juice. Cover and microwave on high for 2–3 minutes until the salmon is opaque all the way through and flakes easily when pressed with a fork.

Alternatively, poach the salmon. Put 500ml (17fl oz) fish or vegetable stock in a medium saucepan and bring up to a simmer. Add the salmon, flesh side down, and cook at a very gentle simmer for 7 minutes. Turn the salmon over and cook for a further 4–5 minutes until the fish is opaque all the way through and breaks into large flakes when pressed with a fork. (Thicker pieces of salmon may take a couple of minutes longer.)

notes

meal planner: feeding you

Below are some healthy meal and snack suggestions for while you're breastfeeding, most of which are drawn from the recipes in this book. These meals should keep your energy levels up and provide you and your baby with essential nutrients.

breakfast	lunch	dinner	extras
Swiss muesli (p29) yogurt	Bag-baked salmon (pp34–35) with broccoli and rice fruit	Hidden vegetable bolognaise (p127) with spaghetti; My favourite frozen yogurt (p134); fruit	Honey and soy toasted seeds (p29) rice cakes
scrambled eggs on wholegrain toast fruit	Hidden vegetable bolognaise (pp126–127) with spaghetti Fruit fool (pp132–133)	Sweet root soup (pp32–33) tomato and mozzarella salad	Sweet root soup (pp32–33) Chicken and avocado wrap (p37) cottage cheese and fruit
cereal and fruit grilled cheese and tomato on toast	Chicken, broccoli, and mangetout pasta salad (p46) Fruit fool (pp132–133)	lamb chops, baked potato, grilled tomato Apple and blackberry surprise (pp172–173)	Muffin pizza (pp152–153) crudités and hummus
porridge with honey or fruit yogurt	Pasta with rocket and mascarpone sauce (p41), salad yogurt	grilled tuna with couscous Bananas "Foster" (p131)	Granola bar (p30) fruit
fruit smoothie boiled egg and toast	Southwestern salad (pp44–45) My favourite frozen yogurt (p134); fruit	Sesame beef and broccoli stir-fry (pp38–39) Orchard crumble (p130)	Turkey and tomato sandwich with honey-mustard mayo (p36) dried apricots
half grapefruit wholegrain toast yoghurt	Frittata provençale (pp42–43) Orchard crumble (p130)	Sweet root soup (pp32–33) grilled chicken or steak fruit	Southwestern salad (pp44–45) Honey and soy toasted seeds (p29)
Swiss muesli (p29) berries	roast chicken or beef with vegetables fruit ice cream	Frittata provençale (pp42–43, with salad Orchard crumble (p130)	Chinese-style beef wrap (p37) cottage cheese fruit

starting solids: 6–9 months

> My aim is to guide you through weaning and preparing the best first foods for your baby. I'll show you how cooking fresh food for your little one can be easy, and you'll have the added benefit of knowing exactly what has gone into it.

first spoonfuls

By around six months your baby's digestive system will be ready for solids and so will her appetite. Weaning can be a daunting time, but it doesn't need to be. I have lots of shortcuts and tips to help you on your way.

The World Health Organization (WHO) guidelines recommend breastfeeding exclusively for the first six months of your baby's life. During this time, in most cases, breast milk or formula provides all the nutrients a baby needs, and should be the only source of nourishment.

● recognizing that she's ready

Don't be in a hurry to wean your baby onto solids. Your baby's digestive and immune systems are not sufficiently developed before she is 17 weeks of age (four months), but the WHO now recommends that it's best not to introduce solids until 26 weeks of age (six months).

By about six months your baby will reach a stage when she needs solid food as well as milk in her diet, for example the iron stores she inherited from you will have been used up, so it's vital to include iron-rich foods in her diet.

There is, however, no "right" age to introduce solids as every baby is different. If you feel that your baby needs solids earlier than six months,

milk matters

How much milk should I give my baby now she is eating solids?

Between 6 and 12 months babies should have a minimum of 500–600ml (17–21fl oz) of milk each day. You can use cow's milk in cooking and with cereals, but breast or formula milk should be your baby's main drink. If your baby drinks less than 500ml (17fl oz) of formula a day or is breastfed beyond six months, she will need supplementary vitamins A, C, and D up until at least one year. These vitamins are in formula milk, but are lower in breast milk. Part of your baby's intake can be from dairy products such as cheese, yogurt, or milk in cooking. If you're breastfeeding, it's not possible to measure the amount of milk your baby is getting, but her growth and your common sense will tell you whether she's getting enough.

ask annabel

my top first foods

* **first fruits:** apple, pear, banana, papaya, and avocado

* **first vegetables:** carrot, potato, swede, parsnip, pumpkin, butternut squash, and sweet potato

* **baby rice:** mix baby rice with water, breast or formula milk, or runny fruit or vegetable purées. Baby rice is easily digested and its milky taste makes an easy transition to solids. Choose one that is sugar free and enriched with vitamins and iron.

speak to your health visitor or GP. Many babies are ready for simple purées, like carrot or apple purée, around five months. I think it's important to follow your instincts because no two babies are the same and mum usually knows best. Here are some signs that your baby is ready to try her first tastes of solid food:

* She is no longer satisfied by a full milk feed.
* She is demanding more frequent milk feeds.
* She is starting to wake at night, when previously she was sleeping through.
* She is starting to show an interest in the things you eat and seems eager to try them herself.

> Most of the time, you can prepare your baby's food alongside the rest of the family's, and weaning a baby presents a great opportunity to make sure the whole family eats well

● the best first foods for your baby

Very first foods should be easy to digest and unlikely to provoke an allergy (for more information on allergies, see pages 14–16 and for advice on which foods to delay giving to your baby, see page 54). I like to begin with root vegetables such as carrots or sweet potato as these have a naturally sweet taste that babies like. Fruits are good for the same reason, but make sure you choose ripe fruits that have a good flavour – it's best to taste them yourself first.

● how to get started

Preparing fresh food for your baby doesn't need to be time-consuming. You can prepare more food than you need and freeze extra individual portions in covered ice cube trays or small plastic pots that are suitable for freezing. By planning ahead with my meal planners (see pages 60–61), you will find that you may need to cook just once or twice a week. Plan your week's shopping and cooking by filling in the blank charts.

Most of the time, you can prepare your baby's food alongside the rest of the family's, and weaning a baby presents a great opportunity to make sure the whole family eats well. If you eat lots of ready meals, it's time to think about making meals from fresh ingredients. If you currently boil vegetables you may want to think about switching to steaming (see box, right). It's easy to steam vegetables while you prepare your own meal – simply leave out the salt, set aside a portion for your baby, and purée it in a blender when your baby is ready for her meal.

tips

Remember to offer your baby foods that you don't like – your baby might enjoy them even if you don't

Steam vegetables. Broccoli loses over 60 per cent of its antioxidants when boiled, but less than 7 per cent when steamed

You can prepare meals for your baby without any cooking. Mash or purée banana, avocado, and papaya

Here are some tips to help you begin weaning:

* **Pick a time of day** when you are not rushed or likely to be distracted and if possible keep to the same time each day (possibly lunchtime), so that you can begin to establish a routine.

* **At the beginning** it may be a good idea to offer food halfway through a milk feed so that your baby isn't frantically hungry or too full.

* **To begin with** you need to get your baby used to something other than milk, so it's important to make very runny purées by adding the boiled water from the base of the steamer, or stir in some of your baby's usual milk. As your baby gets used to solids, you can gradually add less liquid.

* **Heat the food thoroughly**, but then let it cool down to room or lukewarm temperature.

* **Use a shallow soft-tipped weaning spoon** to feed your baby. Some babies may not react well to a spoon, in which case you could dip a scrupulously clean finger into the food and let your baby suck the food off it.

* **Feeding your baby** should be a cosy time – you could hold your baby on your lap with your arm around her or sit her facing you in a bouncy chair.

methods of cooking

* **steaming** is by far the best way to preserve the fresh taste and vitamins in vegetables. Vitamins B and C are water soluble and are easily destroyed by overcooking – especially when boiled.

* **baking** potatoes, sweet potato, and butternut squash gives them a delicious flavour as it caramelizes their natural sugars. It's easy to bake these at the same time as cooking a meal for the family in the oven.

* **boiling** causes vegetables to lose quite a lot of their vitamin content in the water, so I'm not so keen on this method. If you do need to boil vegetables, use the minimum amount of water and add some of the cooking liquid when blending the purée.

* **microwaving** cooks vegetables quickly, requires little water, and doesn't leach out the nutrients into the water, unlike boiling. Some people worry that cooking in a microwave is not good for us, but don't be put off. It is a quick, easy, and safe way to cook as long as you follow the manufacturer's instructions.

● portion size

I am often asked how much food a baby should be eating, but the amount that babies eat varies enormously. The amount of food that one baby needs to eat to maintain the same growth rate can be very different to the next baby – even if they are the same age and weight. Babies have different metabolic rates and activity levels, and the foods that you give them can vary in calorie content, for example a chicken purée will be more filling than a fruit purée. If your baby is growing and seems content then I would let her be the judge.

I recommend feeding a meal until your baby loses interest or until gentle distraction does not regain her interest, and then stopping. Babies are often by nature quite chubby with gorgeous chunky little legs and arms, but these will slim down as your baby becomes more mobile. To be confident that she is receiving all the nutrients she needs, see the nutritional guidelines chart on pages 12–13.

when can I give my baby ... ?

❋ **gluten**, found in wheat, rye, barley, and oats, can be hard for young babies to digest. Foods containing gluten such as bread or pasta should not be introduced before six months.

❋ **honey** should not be given to babies under 12 months as it can cause infant botulism. Although this is very rare, it is best to be safe, as a baby's digestive system is too immature to cope with the bug.

❋ **nuts** For babies with no history of allergy in the family, it is fine to give peanut butter and other finely ground nuts from seven months. However, if there is history of allergy in your family or your baby suffers from eczema, seek medical advice before giving nuts to your baby

(for more advice, see pages 15–16). Whole nuts should not be given before the age of five due to the risk of choking.

❋ **milk** Avoid giving cow's milk as a main drink until your baby is 12 months. However, you can use full-fat cow's milk in cooking and with breakfast cereals from six months. You can give your child semi-skimmed or skimmed milk from the age of two.

❋ **eggs**, cooked until the white and yolk are solid, can be given to your baby from six months. Do not give raw or undercooked eggs before 12 months.

❋ **fish** Both oily and white fish are great for babies from six months, but don't give more

than two portions of oily fish, like salmon or tuna, a week. Shellfish is fine from around nine months.

❋ **cheese** is a nutritious food for your baby from six months. However, you should avoid giving blue cheese and soft unpasteurized cheese, such as Brie, in the first year.

❋ **salt** Babies under one year should not have salt added to their food as this can strain immature kidneys and may cause dehydration. There are other ways to add flavour. See page 65 for advice on this.

❋ **sugar** Unless food is really tart, don't add sugar. Adding sugar is habit-forming and increases the risk of tooth decay.

first vegetable purée

Carrots make excellent weaning food, because babies like their naturally sweet taste. In the first few weeks of weaning, make sure that the carrots are cooked for quite a long time so that they are soft enough to purée. This method of cooking also works for other root vegetables, such as sweet potato, swede, parsnip, and potatoes (cooking times will vary).

- PREPARATION: 5 MINUTES
- COOKING: 15–20 MINUTES STEAMING OR BOILING, OR 9–10 MINUTES MICROWAVING
- MAKES 250ML (9FL OZ)
- PROVIDES BETA-CAROTENE
- SUITABLE FOR FREEZING

350g (12oz) carrots, peeled, washed, and chopped or sliced into even-sized pieces

Steam the carrots for 18–20 minutes until tender. Alternatively, put them in a saucepan, cover with boiling water, and cook, covered, for 15–20 minutes.

To microwave, place the carrots in a suitable dish with 3 tbsp water, and cover, leaving an air vent. Cook on high for 9–10 minutes, stirring halfway through, then leave to stand for 1–2 minutes.

Blend the carrots, with some of the water from the steamer, the cooking liquid, or a little cooled boiled water (or breast or formula milk), to a very smooth purée. The amount of liquid you add depends on your baby – you may need a little more if your baby finds the purée hard to swallow.

date baby first tried ....

baby's reaction ....

what I thought ....

my variations ....

tick reaction

date baby first tried ....

....

baby's reaction ....

....

....

....

what I thought ....

....

....

....

my variations ....

....

....

....

....

....

....

tick
reaction

butternut squash purée

Butternut squash has a naturally sweet flavour that is popular with babies. This is suitable from six months.

- PREPARATION: 8 MINUTES
- COOKING: 15 MINUTES STEAMING OR BOILING, OR 1½ HOURS IN THE OVEN
- MAKES ABOUT 400ML (14FL OZ)
- PROVIDES BETA-CAROTENE
- SUITABLE FOR FREEZING

1 medium butternut squash, peeled, cut in half lengthways, and seeds and fibres removed, then cut into cubes

Melted butter, if baking

Steam the squash cubes, or cover them with boiling water and simmer, for about 15 minutes until tender.

Alternatively, preheat the oven to 200°C (180°C fan), gas 6. Cut the squash in half lengthways, and remove the seeds and fibres. Place the halves, cut side up, in a roasting tin, brush with a little melted butter, and cover loosely with foil. Bake for about 1½ hours until tender. Allow to cool, then scoop out the flesh.

Blend the squash to a purée, then add a little of your baby's usual milk to make a good consistency for your baby.

Variations

Apple and butternut squash purée: peel, core, and chop 2 apples, and put in a saucepan with 4 tbsp water. Cover and simmer for 5 minutes. Blend to a purée and stir into the butternut squash purée. Makes 500ml (17fl oz).

Pear and butternut squash purée: peel, core, and chop 2 ripe pears, and simmer in a small saucepan for 2–3 minutes until soft (juicy ripe pears shouldn't need any extra liquid). Blend to a purée and mix with the butternut squash purée. Makes 500ml (17fl oz).

baked sweet potato purée

Baking sweet potato gives it the best flavour as it caramelizes the natural sugars. Almost any vegetable combined with puréed baked sweet potato will taste delicious (see page 69).

- PREPARATION: 5 MINUTES, PLUS COOLING
- COOKING: 50–60 MINUTES
- MAKES 250ML (9FL OZ)
- PROVIDES CALCIUM, BETA-CAROTENE, FOLATE, VIT B$_6$
- SUITABLE FOR FREEZING

1 medium sweet potato (about 250g/9oz)

100–150ml (3½–5fl oz) milk or boiled water

Preheat the oven to 190°C (170°C fan), gas 5. Wash and lightly scrub the potato, then pierce it in several places with a skewer or prick with a fork. Bake for 50–60 minutes until tender. Allow to cool.

Cut the potato in half and scoop out the flesh. Blend with enough milk or boiled water to make a smooth purée.

date baby first tried ....

baby's reaction ....

what I thought ....

my variations ....

tick reaction

date baby first tried ....

baby's reaction ....

....

....

....

....

what I thought ....

....

....

my variations ....

....

....

....

....

....

....

tick
reaction

apple and pear purée

Both apples and pears make a good first food for babies, because these fruits are unlikely to cause an allergy. Another benefit of these fruits is that they contain the soluble fibre pectin, which helps little bowels to start processing solids efficiently.

- PREPARATION: 5 MINUTES
- COOKING: 6–8 MINUTES
- MAKES 400ML (14FL OZ)
- PROVIDES FOLATE, VITS B_2 & C
- SUITABLE FOR FREEZING

2 eating apples, peeled, cored, and chopped

2 ripe pears, peeled, cored, and chopped

Put the fruit into a heavy-based saucepan with 5 tbsp water. Cover and cook over a low heat for 6–8 minutes until tender. Blend to a smooth purée.

Variations: You can also combine vegetables and fruit by making carrot and apple purée or sweet potato and pear.

no-cook baby foods

Each of the purées below takes no more than a few minutes to prepare, and makes one serving. You can serve them individually, or mix them. Good combinations are avocado and banana; avocado, banana, and yogurt; and papaya and banana.

avocado

Avocados offer the perfect ratio of good fat (monounsaturated), protein, and carbohydrate, all in one food. Being nutrient-dense, they'll help fuel your baby's rapid growth in the first year. Avocado provides folate and vitamins A and B_3.

Cut a small, ripe avocado in half, remove the stone, and scoop out the flesh. Mash half with a little of your baby's usual milk until quite smooth.

banana

Because bananas are easily portable, they are ideal to take with you when you are out and about and want to feed your baby. Banana provides potassium, magnesium, selenium, and folate.

Peel half a small, ripe banana and mash with a fork until quite smooth. You may want to mix the mashed banana with a little of your baby's usual milk to thin down the consistency to begin with.

papaya

Papaya provides beta-carotene, folate, and vitamins B_3, C, and E, and it contains an enzyme that aids digestion.

Cut a small, ripe papaya in half, remove the black seeds, and peel. Mash the flesh of half of the papaya until quite smooth. Alternatively, if the papaya flesh is fibrous, purée in a blender.

date baby first tried ....

baby's reaction ....

what I thought ....

my variations ....

tick reaction

meal planner: first spoonfuls

The meal planner below provides suggestions for your baby's first meals. Use the spaces to record what your baby eats and her milk feeds too. On the opposite page map out your baby's first tastes and record what she eats and drinks.

WEEK 1	first taste	my baby's feeds
day 1	First vegetable purée (p55)	
day 2	Baked sweet potato purée (p57)	
day 3	Apple and pear purée (p58)	
day 4	Banana (p59)	
day 5	First vegetable purée (p55) or Baked sweet potato purée (p57)	
day 6	Butternut squash purée (p56)	
day 7	baby cereal Banana (p59)	

● feeding solids

Simple fruit and vegetable purées are perfect for your baby's first meals. In the early days, you'll need to feed your baby just one meal a day, but this can increase to two by week three.

WEEK 2	first taste	my baby's feeds
day 1		
day 2		
day 3		
day 4		
day 5		
day 6		
day 7		

meal planner: weeks 3 and 4

Use these pages to record the meals and milk feeds you give to your baby over the next weeks. I've provided some suggestions for when you move on to two meals a day. If you want to record your baby's first tastes for longer, simply photocopy these pages.

WEEK 3	breakfast	lunch	my baby's feeds
day 1	pear purée and baby rice	First vegetable purée (p55)	
day 2	apple purée	Butternut squash purée (p56)	
day 3	baby cereal Banana (p59)	carrot and parsnip purée	
day 4	Avocado and Banana (p59)	Apple and butternut squash purée (p56)	
day 5	Papaya (p59) baby cereal	Baked sweet potato purée (p57)	
day 6	Apple and pear purée (p58)	Avocado (p59)	
day 7	baby cereal Banana (p59)	carrot or parsnip and apple purée	

● portion sizes

When you first introduce your baby to solid foods, portion sizes aren't important. A few spoonfuls, once a day, will give her a taste of different flavours and provide a little nutrition.

WEEK 4	breakfast	lunch	my baby's feeds
day 1			
day 2			
day 3			
day 4			
day 5			
day 6			
day 7			

other favourites

Use this page to note down your other favourite recipes, ideas for combinations of different fruits and vegetables, or recipe recommendations from your friends and family. Remember to introduce your baby to new foods one at a time. Enjoy experimenting!

new tastes

Once your baby is comfortable with the simple purées, you can begin to introduce more flavours. With your guidance, your baby will be excited to discover that foods have different tastes and new textures.

The needs of babies and toddlers are different to those of adults. Low-fat, high-fibre diets are great for adults but not appropriate for babies or young children who need more fat and concentrated sources of calories and nutrients to fuel their rapid growth. Babies shouldn't be given too much fibre as it tends to be bulky and can fill them up before they get all the nutrients they need for proper growth and development. Excess fibre can hinder the absorption of vital nutrients and can cause other problems such as diarrhoea.

Babies should continue to eat a wide variety of fruit and vegetables. However, after the first few weeks of weaning, you can begin to offer your baby foods that are higher in calories such as mashed avocado, fruit mixed with Greek yogurt, or vegetables in a cheese sauce.

● fruit

At six months, your baby should be able to eat most fruits. However, there are a few fruits that give babies upset tummies or can cause a reaction. To begin with, it is best to give only small amounts of citrus fruits (such as oranges), berries (for example strawberries), and kiwi fruits to your baby as they can cause redness around the mouth, especially in babies and children with eczema. This is an irritant effect, and rarely due to allergy.

experiment with flavours

✳ **combine ingredients** to make interesting flavours. Don't be afraid to mix sweet with savoury. Fruit with puréed chicken or fish, for example, is a favourite with many babies. Try your baby with lots of different combinations.

✳ **add garlic**. As you can't add salt to babies' food before one year, I like to use garlic to add flavour. Garlic is very healthy – in fact, the Greeks and Romans ate it before going to war as they believed it made them strong. Allicin, which gives off the strong smell, helps to kill off nasty bacteria and viruses. Eaten regularly, garlic can help to prevent colds.

✳ **herbs**, like fresh thyme and basil, are another great way to add flavour without adding salt.

Dried fruits are fine in moderation, but be careful, as too many can have a laxative effect. Choose dried apricots that are not treated with sulphur dioxide (E220) – this is used to preserve their bright orange colour and can trigger an asthma attack in susceptible babies.

● vegetables

At six months, your baby can eat all vegetables, but stronger tasting vegetables like spinach are best mixed with root vegetables such as sweet potato. Frozen vegetables are frozen within hours of being picked, thus sealing in all the nutrients, and can be more nutritious than fresh, so it is absolutely fine to use frozen peas or spinach when making baby food.

● breads and cereals

From six months, your baby can have gluten, so you can ditch the baby rice and give cereals like soaked muesli and porridge. You can also offer rice cakes, toast fingers, pita bread, or halved bagels to your baby from around eight months.

● dairy

Although you should wait until your baby is 12 months to introduce cow's milk as a drink, it can be used with cereal and in cooking from six months. Yogurts and fromage frais are popular but choose the full-fat rather than low-fat varieties, and check the label as they can often be high in sugar.

It is good to add cheese to vegetables or fish as it's rich in calcium and protein, and provides the calories that babies need for their rapid growth. Cheddar, Parmesan, ricotta, and cream cheese are all great choices.

● meat

Iron is very important for your baby's mental and physical development. A baby is born with a store

drink dilemma

Should I give my baby juice or water to drink as well as milk?

Water is the best drink for babies under 12 months. If your baby is less than six months, boil mains tap water and allow it to cool before giving it to him. Bottled mineral water is unsuitable for young babies as it contains high levels of mineral salts. If your baby is on a vegetarian diet, then it's a good idea to give a vitamin C-rich fruit juice with meals, as this helps him to absorb iron from his food. All babies can have a little unsweetened juice, but dilute it with at least three parts water to one part juice. Too much juice can cause diarrhoea. Drinks with added sugar or artificial sweeteners are unsuitable. It's best to give juice in a cup and put only milk or water in his bottle. Introduce a two-handled beaker as soon as he's ready to hold one.

ask annabel

tips

Remember to check the labels. Baby rusks and yogurts can be high in sugar

Cooking fish in a microwave is a great option when you're pushed for time, as it takes just a few minutes to cook

Avoid blue cheese before 12 months as the strong moulds can upset little tummies

of iron that lasts for about six months. After this it is important that your baby obtains the iron she needs from her diet. Iron in foods of animal origin such as red meat or poultry is much better absorbed than iron in foods of plant origin like green vegetables or cereal. Pork and lamb are lower in iron than beef, and liver is the best source of iron. When giving babies chicken choose the brown meat as well as the breast as it contains twice as much iron and zinc as the white meat. Good non-meat sources of iron include pulses, fortified wholegrain cereals, and leafy green vegetables.

fish

It is hard to find jars of purée containing fish, which is why making fish dishes for your baby is especially important. Fish is an excellent food for babies and combines well with a cheese sauce. Oily fish, such as salmon, trout, fresh tuna, and sardines, is rich in essential fatty acids (EFAs), and I can't stress enough how important these are for the development of your baby's brain, vision, and nervous system. Ideally you should give your baby oily fish twice a week, but no more, as there are concerns over the build-up of toxins in the body. Alternative sources of EFAs for babies on vegetarian diets are soya bean products.

It's important not to overcook fish. Check the fish carefully with clean fingers to make sure that there are no bones.

eggs

Eggs are very nutritious and fine for your baby to eat from six months as long as the white and yolk are cooked until solid. Eggs from chickens that have been fed an omega-3-rich diet are also another great source of EFAs. If there is history of allergy in the family or your baby suffers from eczema, your baby is more likely to suffer from an egg allergy. Consult your doctor if you're concerned.

baby's likes and dislikes

Don't be surprised if your baby shows taste preferences at this early age. Babies have well-developed taste buds and have likes and dislikes just like adults. Every baby is different. If she rejects a food, try serving it again in a few weeks – she may have changed her mind.

If your baby does have a particular favourite, it's best not to offer it all the time. Introducing a wide variety of tastes, colours, and textures is especially important in your baby's first year so she learns to accept a variety of foods and does not become fixed in her food preferences.

date baby first tried ....

baby's reaction ....
....
....
....
....

what I thought ....
....
....
....

my variations ....
....
....
....
....
....
....
....

tick
reaction

tasty vegetable trio

Nutritionists and scientists agree that broccoli is truly a miraculous vegetable – a powerhouse of antioxidants. The best way to cook it is by lightly steaming it, or microwaving it in very little water, because when boiled it can lose more than 50 per cent of its vitamin C content.

- PREPARATION: 10 MINUTES
- COOKING: 20 MINUTES
- MAKES 450ML (15FL OZ)
- PROVIDES PROTEIN, CALCIUM, FOLATE, BETA-CAROTENE, VITS B_{12}, C, & D
- SUITABLE FOR FREEZING

3 medium carrots (about 200g/7oz), peeled and sliced

60g (generous 2oz) broccoli florets

25g (scant 1oz) butter

2 medium, ripe tomatoes (about 200g/7oz), skinned, deseeded, and cut into pieces

50g (scant 2oz) Cheddar cheese, grated

Steam the carrots for 10 minutes, then add the broccoli (ideally use a two-tiered steamer) and continue to steam for 7 minutes until tender.

Melt the butter in a pan and sauté the tomatoes for 2–3 minutes until mushy. Remove from the heat and stir in the cheese until melted. Add the carrots and broccoli and blend to a purée in the pan using an electric hand blender, adding a little of the steaming liquid for a runnier consistency.

Variation: Use cauliflower instead of broccoli.

sweet potato and spinach purée

A good way to introduce stronger-tasting green vegetables to your baby is to mix them with root vegetables. Baked sweet potato is particularly good as a base, because baking this vegetable accentuates its sweetness. It's worth popping some sweet potatoes into the oven when you are making a roast for the rest of the family.

- PREPARATION: 6 MINUTES, PLUS COOLING
- COOKING: ABOUT 55 MINUTES
- MAKES 275ML (9½FL OZ)
- PROVIDES CALCIUM, BETA-CAROTENE, VITS A, C, & D
- SUITABLE FOR FREEZING

50g (scant 2oz) fresh baby spinach leaves, carefully washed

A generous knob of butter

1 sweet potato (about 250g/9oz), baked and cooled (see page 57)

125ml (4fl oz) milk

Put the washed spinach into a pan and cook for about 3 minutes until wilted. Remove the spinach from the pan and press out any excess liquid. Melt the butter in the pan and sauté the spinach for 1 minute.

Halve the baked sweet potato and scoop out the flesh, then blend with the sautéed spinach and milk to a purée.

date baby first tried ....

baby's reaction ....

....

....

....

....

what I thought ....

....

....

my variations ....

....

....

....

....

....

tick reaction

date baby first tried ....

....

baby's reaction ....

....

....

....

what I thought ....

....

....

my variations ....

....

....

....

....

....

....

tick
reaction

porridge with apple, pear, and apricot

This makes a nutritious breakfast and is suitable from six months. Pack up portions of the fruit purée and freeze. Then you can thaw them overnight, ready to mix with your baby's porridge in the morning. As your baby gets older, you can simply stir in rather than purée.

- PREPARATION: 8 MINUTES
- COOKING: 8 MINUTES
- MAKES 400ML (14FL OZ) FRUIT PURÉE (2–3 TBSP PER PORTION OF PORRIDGE)
- PROVIDES CALCIUM, IRON, FOLATE, BETA-CAROTENE, VIT C, PREBIOTICS
- FRUIT PURÉE SUITABLE FOR FREEZING

1 apple, peeled, cored, and chopped

1 ripe pear, peeled, cored, and chopped

4 ready-to-eat dried apricots, chopped

To serve (per portion)

6 tbsp milk

1 heaped tbsp porridge oats

Put the fruit into a saucepan with 4 tbsp water. Cover and cook for about 6 minutes until tender. Allow to cool, then blend to a purée.

To make the porridge, combine the milk and oats in another small saucepan. Bring to the boil, then simmer, stirring occasionally, for about 3 minutes. Combine the fruit and the porridge, and blend to a purée.

my first beef casserole

I like to introduce red meat to babies soon after six months as their store of iron inherited from their mother runs out at around this age, and red meat provides the richest source of iron. The best way to prepare red meat for babies is to cook it slowly with root vegetables.

- PREPARATION: 10 MINUTES
- COOKING: 1 HOUR
- MAKES 600ML (1 PINT)
- PROVIDES PROTEIN, IRON, POTASSIUM, SELENIUM, ZINC, BETA-CAROTENE, PREBIOTICS
- SUITABLE FOR FREEZING

1 tbsp olive oil

1 small red onion, chopped

1 clove garlic, crushed

¼ tsp fresh thyme leaves or a pinch of dried thyme

125g (4½oz) lean stewing steak, cut into chunks

2 tsp tomato purée

1 large sweet potato (about 225g/8oz), peeled and chopped

2 potatoes (about 275g/10oz), peeled and chopped

250ml (9fl oz) chicken stock

Heat the oil in a flameproof casserole and sauté the onion over a low heat for about 5 minutes until softened. Add the garlic and thyme, and cook for 1 more minute. Add the stewing steak and sauté for a few minutes until seared. Add in the tomato purée and sauté for 1 minute, stirring.

Add the sweet potato and potatoes, and pour over the chicken stock. Bring to the boil, then cover and simmer, stirring occasionally, for about 50 minutes until the meat is very tender. You may need to add a little extra stock during cooking. Leave to cool slightly, then blend to a purée.

> Often it's the texture rather than the taste of red meat that babies object to. Mixing beef with root vegetables and cooking it slowly gives it a soft texture that babies like

date baby first tried ....

baby's reaction ....

what I thought ....

my variations ....

tick reaction

date baby first tried ....

baby's reaction ....
....
....
....

what I thought ....
....
....

my variations ....
....
....
....
....
....
....

tick
reaction

my favourite chicken purée

This is very tasty and a good introduction to chicken. Adding a little sweetness by combining the chicken with sweet potato and dried apricots makes it appealing to babies. I've used chicken thigh as it has a softer, more moist consistency than breast, and the dark meat of chicken has twice as much iron and zinc as the white.

- PREPARATION: 10 MINUTES
- COOKING: 25 MINUTES
- MAKES 600ML (1 PINT)
- PROVIDES PROTEIN, IRON, SELENIUM, ZINC, BETA-CAROTENE, VIT C
- SUITABLE FOR FREEZING

2 chicken thighs

1 tbsp olive oil

50g (scant 2oz) sliced leek

225g (8oz) peeled and chopped sweet potato

40g (scant 1½oz) dried apricots, halved

150ml (5fl oz) passata

200ml (7fl oz) chicken stock or water

Remove the meat from the chicken thighs and discard the skin and fat. I use about 110g (4oz) chicken thigh meat for this recipe. Cut into chunks.
  Heat the oil in a pan and sauté the leek for about 4 minutes until softened. Add the chicken and sauté for about 2 minutes until the chunks are white on all sides. Add the sweet potato and sauté for 1 minute. Stir in the dried apricots, passata, and chicken stock. Bring to the boil, then cover and simmer for about 15 minutes. Blend to a purée.

potato and carrot mash with salmon

It's hard to find jars of baby purée with oily fish like salmon, which is the best source of essential fatty acids that are vital for your baby's brain and visual development. Mashed potato and carrot mixed with a little milk, butter, and cheese makes a good base for a baby's meal. I prefer to mash potato, because puréeing it in a blender breaks down the natural starches, leaving a gloopy texture. If mashed food is too lumpy for your baby, you could try using a baby food grinder or potato ricer to prepare this.

- PREPARATION: 10 MINUTES
- COOKING: 20 MINUTES
- MAKES 400ML (14FL OZ)
- PROVIDES PROTEIN, OMEGA-3s, CALCIUM, IRON, SELENIUM, BETA-CAROTENE, VITS A & D
- SUITABLE FOR FREEZING

300g (10½oz) potatoes, peeled and chopped

100g (3½oz) carrot, peeled and sliced

3½ tbsp milk

Generous knob of butter

40g (scant 1½oz) Cheddar cheese, grated

100g (3½oz) piece of salmon fillet, skinned

Put the potatoes and carrot into a saucepan, cover with boiling water, and cook for 20 minutes until the vegetables are tender. Drain and mash together with 3 tbsp milk, the butter, and cheese.

While the vegetables are cooking, put the salmon into a suitable microwave dish with the remaining ½ tbsp milk, and microwave on high for 1½ minutes. (If you don't have a microwave, you can steam the fish over the vegetables for 5–6 minutes.) Flake the fish, checking to make sure that there are no bones in it.

Mix the fish into the potato and carrot mash.

date baby first tried ....

baby's reaction ....

what I thought ....

my variations ....

tick reaction

fillet of fish with cheesy vegetable sauce

This makes a good introduction to fish for your baby. Plaice is one of the best fish to start with as it has a lovely moist, soft texture. I like to boost the nutrients in the cheese sauce by adding steamed carrot and broccoli, which are rich in vitamins. If you don't have a microwave, you can poach the fillet of plaice in a small saucepan of milk instead.

- PREPARATION: 8 MINUTES
- COOKING: 15 MINUTES
- MAKES 350ML (12FL OZ)
- PROVIDES PROTEIN, CALCIUM, IRON, SELENIUM, BETA-CAROTENE, VITS A, B_{12}, C, & D
- SUITABLE FOR FREEZING

1 medium carrot, peeled and sliced

40g (scant 1½oz) broccoli florets

1 fillet of plaice (or other white fish fillet), skinned (about 100g/3½oz)

A knob of butter

Sauce

15g (½oz) butter

15g (½oz) plain flour

150ml (5fl oz) milk

40g (scant 1½oz) Cheddar cheese, grated

Steam the carrot for 5 minutes, then add the broccoli florets and continue to steam for about 7 minutes until the vegetables are tender. Meanwhile, put the plaice into a suitable microwave dish, dot with butter, and microwave on high for about 1½ minutes.

To make the cheese sauce, melt the butter, stir in the flour, and cook over a low heat for 1 minute. Gradually whisk in the milk. Bring to the boil and simmer for a few minutes until thickened and smooth. Remove from the heat and stir in the grated cheese until melted.

Blend the vegetables and flaked fish with the cheese sauce to a purée.

Note: As your baby gets older, you can mash the vegetables and fish with the sauce, rather than making a purée.

meal planner: new tastes

This meal planner provides suggestions for your baby's meals, many of which are drawn from this book. Either use the planner pages to map out your baby's meals for the next weeks or to keep a record of your baby's diet week-by-week.

breakfast	lunch	dinner	extras
Porridge with apple, pear, and apricot (p70)	My favourite chicken purée (p72)	First vegetable purée (p55) or Baked sweet potato purée (p57)	After the savoury purée at lunch and dinner, you can give your baby a fruit purée or yogurt. Introduce new foods such as mango, peach, and cantaloupe melon – these don't need cooking and can be served alone or with baby rice or banana.
apple or mango purée and cereal	My favourite chicken purée (p72)	Tasty vegetable trio (p68)	
Banana (p59) or mashed peach and banana cereal	Fillet of fish with cheesy vegetable sauce (pp74–75)	Tasty vegetable trio (p68)	
Porridge with apple, pear, and apricot (p70) yogurt	Fillet of fish with cheesy vegetable sauce (pp74–75)	Sweet potato and spinach purée (p69)	
pear purée and baby rice yogurt	My first beef casserole (p71)	Sweet potato and spinach purée (p69)	
Avocado and Banana (p59) cereal	My first beef casserole (p71)	Butternut squash purée (p56)	
Apple and pear purée (p58) cereal	Potato and carrot mash with salmon (p73)	My favourite chicken purée (p72)	

● a varied diet

Even at this young age, your baby doesn't need to eat the same things every day. Vary breakfasts with different fruit purées and serve with porridge, cereal, or baby rice.

WEEK 1	breakfast	lunch	dinner	extras
day 1				
day 2				
day 3				
day 4				
day 5				
day 6				
day 7				

meal planner: weeks 2 and 3

Use these planners to record the meals you give your baby over the following weeks. If you want to record your baby's meals for longer than three weeks, simply photocopy this page. Keep note of your baby's milk feeds too, if you wish.

WEEK 2	breakfast	lunch	dinner	extras
day 1				
day 2				
day 3				
day 4				
day 5				
day 6				
day 7				

● **experiment with flavours**
Try your baby with different combinations of
first foods such as apple and pear (p58) or
carrot and parsnip. Mix fruit and vegetables
too, such as apple and butternut squash (p56).

WEEK 3	breakfast	lunch	dinner	extras
day 1				
day 2				
day 3				
day 4				
day 5				
day 6				
day 7				

other favourites

Use this page to note down your other favourite recipes, ideas for combinations of different fruits and vegetables, or recipe recommendations from your friends and family. Remember to introduce your baby to new foods one at a time. Enjoy experimenting!

older babies: 9–12 months

" Your child is changing from a baby to a mini person and it's no surprise that he'll soon prefer to feed himself. Finger foods are popular and I've provided you with tasty and nutritious recipes that are perfect for little fingers. "

fingers and spoons

Towards the end of the first year, a baby's weight gain tends to slow down dramatically. This is a time of growing independence and often babies who have been good eaters in the past become more difficult to feed.

By around nine months you'll notice that your baby may prefer to feed himself. He'll probably let you know that he's ready by grabbing the spoon you're feeding him with or snatching food off your plate. By doing this, your baby learns about food's texture, smell, and flavour, so it's important to give him an assortment of foods and let him try.

textures

You begin to think everything is going swimmingly with your baby slurping his way through your puréed carrots and sweet potato; then you ditch the blender and it all goes pear-shaped. The transition from perfectly puréed to lumpy food can be difficult as many babies are lazy about chewing, but it's important to give your baby grated, mashed, and chopped food. The muscles a baby uses to chew are the same ones used for speech, so encouraging your baby to chew will help his speech development too.

I would recommend stirring tiny soft lumps, like pasta stars or mini pasta shells, into your baby's favourite purées, gradually increasing the texture and lumpiness of his food. Couscous is another good food; it's a form of grain made from wheat and you can find it in most supermarkets next to the rice. It's quick to prepare and nice and soft, so it acts as a gradual transition from purées to a more lumpy texture and it is tasty with diced vegetables or chicken.

finger foods

This can be a stressful time for parents, as babies find it hard to cope with more lumpy food and generally prefer to feed themselves than be fed. Interestingly, while many babies refuse anything with lumps in it, they will often happily chew on

finger foods such as cucumber sticks or pieces of fruit. Around eight or nine months, as your child's hand to eye coordination matures, finger foods will become an increasingly important part of his diet. Your baby's aim will be far from perfect, but the more you allow him to experiment, the quicker he will learn to feed himself.

● savoury finger foods

To begin with, it's best to give steamed vegetables rather than raw. Your baby may be able to bite off a piece of raw carrot and then be unable to chew, so there is a risk of choking. Try steamed carrot sticks or broccoli florets. Later on your baby will become more proficient at chewing, and you can give him raw vegetables. Many babies prefer to be given a whole carrot or chunk of cucumber to chew on, rather than chopping them into small pieces. Other ideas include rice cakes, bread sticks, and pieces of avocado.

● fruity finger foods

Fresh fruit makes perfect finger food, but do be careful not to give fruits with stones or whole grapes, as these may cause your baby to choke. Try cutting up a selection of fruits, lay them out on a tray, and let your child pick them up and dunk them into a tasty dip. Begin with soft fruits like banana, pear, or peach. Wedges of cantaloupe melon, slices of peeled pear or apple, or grapes cut in half are also good. Try dried apricots too – they are a great source of fibre, iron, and vitamins.

● something cool for sore gums

During the three months up to your baby's first birthday, he may cut several teeth and sore gums may put him off eating. It's a good idea to pop something cool like cucumber sticks in the fridge, as chewing on something cold can be very soothing. Another idea is to freeze a banana for 20 minutes, unpeel it, and let your baby suck on it.

mealtime mayhem

I'm worried that my baby will never have good table manners – she throws food everywhere. Is there anything I can do?

This is an age when children experiment with their food, and if you are the type of person who likes everything neat and tidy you are going to have to draw a deep breath, as your child is going to want to play with her food. She's going to want to touch, hold, and occasionally drop her food. The more you allow her to experiment, the quicker she'll learn to feed herself. Allow her to explore the feel of food and take time over eating it. It may be a messy time, but you should not discourage her attempts or worry about her table manners. She will pick up on your anxieties and mealtimes will turn into a battleground. See opposite page for tips on dealing with mess.

ask annabel

tips

Your baby's hands should always be washed before and after eating

Put a little petroleum jelly around your baby's mouth and chin if he dribbles while teething to prevent any soreness

As your baby starts to crawl he will need more energy-rich foods, such as meat, chicken, cheese, pasta, and dried fruit

You could also try making your own healthy fresh fruit ice lollies. You can purée fruits like peaches or mangoes and mix them with orange or tropical fruit juice or purée, and sieve berry fruits and mix them with strawberry drinking yogurt. Alternatively, simply pour fresh fruit juice or a smoothie into an ice lolly mould and freeze. See pages 135–137 for recipes for ice lollies and smoothie sticks.

Other good foods for babies during teething include yogurt, fruit purées, jelly, and risotto.

● mini meals

Babies have small stomachs and cannot take in too much at each mealtime, so they need light meals that are full of protein and slow-releasing carbohydrates. There are some great finger foods that supply everything they need. Try the delicious Salmon fishcakes (pages 98–99), Poached chicken balls (page 101), and Goujons of fish (page 115). A favourite with my children is Tuna tortilla melt (page 119).

● encouraging healthy eating

At this age children are fascinated by what older children and adults are doing, so it is important that your baby is surrounded by people eating normal, healthy meals. Try to sit alongside your baby and eat your own lunch while you feed him. Invite another mum and baby round occasionally – especially if the baby is a good eater.

● dealing with mess

Mealtimes are going to get messy, so it's a good idea to put a large plastic splash or mess mat under the highchair to catch the food that falls on the floor. Other useful pieces of equipment include a spoon and fork set that is attached to the highchair tray or to the table with a curly wire – so that even if your baby flings the cutlery down, it doesn't drop on the floor. A bowl with a strong suction base is also a great purchase.

There is no need to be obsessive about germs. It's fine to use an antibacterial wipe to clean your baby's highchair but, remember, your baby picks things up from the floor and puts them in his mouth all the time.

One very common thing that paediatric dieticians talk about is children who are afraid of mess. This seems to be at the root of many toddler eating problems. Allow your baby to experiment – he's bound to get himself into a mess, but it's not a good idea to continually wipe your child's face clean when he is eating.

● choking

Usually, babies gag, cough, or spit food out if they cannot swallow it. However, you should always stay with your baby when he's feeding himself in case he chokes. Just because your child can chew off a piece of food, like a piece of toast, it doesn't mean that he can chew it properly. Sometimes babies chew off pieces of food and then store them in their mouths, so always check when you lift your child out of the highchair that there is no lumpy food left in his mouth. When my children were babies, I sometimes found that they would keep food in their mouths long after I thought they had finished. Check that your baby has swallowed everything before you leave the room – especially if you are just starting him on hard finger foods.

* **If your child chokes,** don't try to retrieve the food with your fingers, as this can push it further down the windpipe.

* **Lay your baby face down** on your forearm, with his head lower than his body. Give him five sharp slaps across the top of his back between his shoulder blades. Pick out any visible obstructions with your forefinger and thumb.

* **If the obstruction is still present,** turn your baby over on to his back and give five sharp thrusts, at a rate of one every three seconds, pushing down with two fingers in the middle of his chest. Then check your baby's mouth again for any obstruction.

* **If unsuccessful, repeat the sequence** and call emergency services immediately.

finger food ideas

* **vegetables,** such as broccoli, carrots, cauliflower, parsnip, and asparagus. Lightly steam or boil them at first so they are a little crunchy, but not hard. Once your baby is more proficient at chewing, you can give him raw vegetables. Other tasty ideas include halved cherry tomatoes and slices of avocado.

* **fruit** such as banana chunks, apple, peach, melon, or pear slices. Soft fruits are best at first if your baby finds it difficult to chew. Serve with a tasty dip.

* **dried fruit,** for example dried apricots, figs, prunes, or large pieces of apple. Be careful with smaller pieces, such as raisins, as your baby may choke.

* **mini sandwiches** with soft fillings (see pages 90–92).

* **starchy finger foods** such as fingers of toast, mini rice cakes, rusks, bread sticks, strips of pita bread.

* **dry cereals** are very handy when you're on the go. Avoid the sugar-coated varieties, though.

* **cold, cooked pasta shapes** are great energy-boosters.

* **cheese cut into sticks, or cheese slices or mini cheeses.**

* **protein-rich finger foods** such as chicken balls (see page 101 for recipe) or salmon fishcakes (see page 99), or small pieces of cooked chicken or turkey.

* **lollies and smoothie sticks,** (see pages 135–137 for recipes), jelly, and yogurt are all soothing for your baby during teething.

finger foods my baby has tried

Finger foods encourage self-feeding and give your baby a sense of independence. Try to include some at each meal. See the ideas on the opposite page and record which ones your baby has tried and enjoyed and which ones he disliked.

date baby first tried ....

baby's reaction ....

....

....

....

what I thought ....

....

....

my variations ....

....

....

....

....

....

....

tick
reaction

my first muesli

Baby porridge oats are nice and fine so make a good base on which to add extra – and new – textures.

- PREPARATION: 4–5 MINUTES
- COOKING: NONE
- MAKES 1 PORTION
- PROVIDES POTASSIUM, CALCIUM, VITS A, B_1, B_3, & D, PREBIOTICS

2 tbsp baby porridge oats

2 tbsp milk (or breast milk or formula)

1 tbsp strawberry or vanilla yogurt

½ small banana, mashed or diced

Mix the oats, milk, and yogurt together, then stir in the banana. Add a little extra milk if your baby likes a runnier consistency.

french toast fingers

Cinnamon raisin bread makes a nice alternative to ordinary bread for French toast (also called pain perdu or eggy bread) – it reminds me of bread and butter pudding. If you don't have any handy then you can simply add a good pinch of cinnamon to the egg mixture and serve the French toast with a few raisins. Flattening the bread makes it easier for small mouths to chew.

- PREPARATION: 5 MINUTES
- COOKING: 4–5 MINUTES
- MAKES 1 PORTION
- PROVIDES IRON, SELENIUM, VITS D & E

1 small slice cinnamon raisin bread

1 egg yolk

1 tsp cream (or milk)

1–2 drops of pure vanilla extract

Pinch of caster sugar

15g (½oz) butter

Flatten the bread by rolling it out with a rolling pin until it is about half of its original thickness. Beat the egg yolk, cream, vanilla extract, and sugar together in a flat dish.

Melt the butter in a frying pan over a medium heat. When the butter is foaming, dip the bread into the egg mixture, then fry in the hot butter for about 2 minutes on each side until golden. Allow to cool until warm, then serve cut into fingers.

Note: To make two portions, use a whole egg and double everything else.

> "You can also make French toast using white bread or challah (Jewish egg bread). Slices of grilled cheese on toast make a delicious breakfast for older babies too"

date baby first tried ....

baby's reaction ....

what I thought ....

my variations ....

tick reaction

finger food sandwiches

The trick to good sandwiches is not to have too much bread or too much filling. I like to flatten the bread by rolling with a rolling pin so that the sandwich is easier for small children to eat. For toddlers it is best to cut the sandwich into bite-size pieces, but as your child gets older it is fun to cut the sandwiches into fingers or other shapes.

tasty tuna

I find that tuna packed in olive oil has a slightly nicer flavour, but you can use tuna packed in water if you prefer. Older children may like ½ tbsp drained sweetcorn added to the mix.

- PREPARATION: 8 MINUTES
- COOKING: NONE
- MAKES 1–2 PORTIONS
- PROVIDES PROTEIN, IRON, ZINC, VIT C

55g (2oz) drained tinned tuna (about ⅓ tin)

1 tbsp mayonnaise

1 tsp tomato ketchup

Salt and pepper

2 slices bread, flattened

Put the tuna in a bowl and mash it well, then stir in the mayonnaise and ketchup. Season to taste with salt and pepper. Spread on one slice of bread and sandwich with the other slice. Cut into squares or fingers.

"cream tea"

I like raspberry jam as it is devoid of lumps, which can put a toddler off his sandwich. However, you can use your favourite jam or marmalade.

- PREPARATION: 5 MINUTES
- COOKING: NONE
- MAKES 1–2 PORTIONS
- PROVIDES PROTEIN, CALCIUM, VIT D

2 tbsp cream cheese, at room temperature

2 slices bread, flattened

1½ tsp raspberry jam

Spread 1 tbsp of cream cheese on to each slice of bread. Spread the jam on top of one slice and top with the remaining slice. Cut into squares or fingers.

double cheese sandwich

If your child likes yeast extract then you can use ¼–½ tsp instead of the ketchup. These are also nice as open-face sandwiches – just use Cheddar cheese and only half of the cream cheese base.

- PREPARATION: 8 MINUTES
- COOKING: NONE
- MAKES 1–2 PORTIONS
- PROVIDES PROTEIN, CALCIUM, VIT D

2 tbsp cream cheese

1½ tsp tomato ketchup

2 slices bread, flattened

30g (1oz) Cheddar cheese, thinly sliced or grated

Mix the cream cheese and ketchup together in a small bowl. Spread half on to each slice of bread. Top one slice with the cheese and sandwich with the remaining slice. Cut into squares or fingers.

cream cheese and banana sandwich

This is also nice spread on toast for breakfast.

- PREPARATION: 5 MINUTES
- COOKING: NONE
- MAKES 1–2 PORTIONS
- PROVIDES PROTEIN, POTASSIUM, CALCIUM, VIT D

2 tbsp cream cheese

1 tsp maple syrup (or clear honey for babies over one year)

½ small banana, mashed

2 slices bread, flattened

Mix the cream cheese and maple syrup (or honey) together in a bowl, then stir in the banana. Spread on to one slice of bread and sandwich with the remaining slice. Cut into squares or fingers.

broccoli and cheese baby bites

This is essentially a broccoli and cheese purée, bound with fresh breadcrumbs. It makes good finger food rolled into small balls and coated in crumbs and fried – many babies at this age refuse to be fed with a spoon. You must chill the balls well before cooking.

- PREPARATION: 30 MINUTES, PLUS AT LEAST 1 HOUR CHILLING
- COOKING: 2–3 MINUTES PER BATCH
- MAKES ABOUT 20 (3–4 PER PORTION)
- PROVIDES PROTEIN, CALCIUM, FOLATE, VITS A, C, & D
- SUITABLE FOR FREEZING

110g (4oz) broccoli florets

4 slices white bread, crusts removed

30g (1oz) mature Cheddar cheese, grated

30g (1oz) mozzarella cheese, grated

1–2 eggs, beaten

3 tbsp dried breadcrumbs

3 tbsp freshly grated Parmesan cheese

1 tbsp plain flour

3–4 tbsp sunflower oil, for frying

Steam the broccoli florets for 7–8 minutes until soft. Transfer them to a plate and allow to cool.

Put the bread in a food processor and whiz to crumbs, then tip into a bowl. Put the broccoli, Cheddar, and mozzarella in the food processor and whiz until puréed. Add to the breadcrumbs and squish everything together until well combined. (The mixture may need a little liquid to help it bind, in which case add 1–2 tsp of the beaten egg.)

Mix the dried breadcrumbs and Parmesan on a large plate. Put the flour on another plate and the beaten egg in a bowl. Roll teaspoonfuls of the broccoli mixture into small balls. Dust with flour, then dip in the egg and, finally, roll in the breadcrumbs. Leave to set in the fridge for at least 1 hour or, preferably, overnight.

Heat the oil in a non-stick frying pan and cook the balls over a high heat, turning frequently, for 2–3 minutes until golden brown all over. Drain on kitchen paper and allow to cool to warm before serving.

Note: The bites can be kept in the fridge for 2–3 days and then cooked when needed. To freeze, open freeze, then transfer to plastic bags; cook from frozen, adding an extra minute to the cooking time.

date baby first tried ....

baby's reaction ....

what I thought ....

my variations ....

tick reaction

> Broccoli is king of the superstar vegetables. It is one of the richest sources of disease-fighting antioxidants. Try to sneak it on to your child's plate whenever possible

date baby first tried ....

baby's reaction ....

....

....

....

what I thought ....

....

....

my variations ....

....

....

....

....

....

tick
reaction

"A good way to encourage your baby to chew is to stir mini pasta shapes into his favourite purées. Chewing also helps develop the muscles for speech"

tomato, sweet potato, and cheese sauce with pasta shells

This delicious sauce is fairly thick and enriched with vegetables. It is very versatile. You can mix it with pasta, as here, or blend it together with vegetables, fish, or chicken.

- PREPARATION: 10 MINUTES
- COOKING: 30 MINUTES
- MAKES 8 PORTIONS OF SAUCE
- PROVIDES PROTEIN, CALCIUM, BETA-CAROTENE, VITS B_6, C, D, & E, PREBIOTICS
- SAUCE SUITABLE FOR FREEZING

1 tbsp olive oil

1 onion, chopped

1 clove garlic, crushed

225g (8oz) sweet potato, peeled and chopped

2 medium carrots, peeled and sliced

1 x 400g (14oz) tin chopped tomatoes

200ml (7fl oz) boiling vegetable stock or water

55g (2oz) Cheddar cheese, grated

To serve

Mini pasta shells (25g/scant 1oz for each portion of sauce)

Heat the oil in a saucepan and sauté the onion for about 4 minutes until softened. Add the garlic and sauté for 1 more minute. Stir in the sweet potato and carrots, then pour in the tomatoes and boiling vegetable stock or water. Bring to the boil, stirring, then cover the pan and simmer for about 30 minutes until the vegetables are tender.

Allow to cool slightly, then blend the sauce to a purée and stir in the cheese until melted.

Cook the pasta according to the instructions on the packet. Drain the pasta and mix with the sauce.

perfectly poached chicken

I usually have cooked chicken in my fridge as it is a handy standby for snacks and meals (see below). Poaching is a nice way of cooking chicken breast as it helps to keep it moist.

- PREPARATION: 2 MINUTES
- COOKING: 20–25 MINUTES
- MAKES 4 PORTIONS
- PROVIDES PROTEIN, IRON, ZINC, SELENIUM

150g (5½oz) skinless, boneless chicken breast

600–750ml (1–1¼ pints) chicken stock

Put the chicken breast in a saucepan and add enough stock to cover. Put the pan over a medium heat and bring to the boil, then reduce the heat to a very low simmer and poach the chicken for 15 minutes. Turn the breast over and cook for a further 5–10 minutes until the chicken is thoroughly cooked. To check, make a small cut in the side of the chicken breast and peek in to make sure the meat has turned white all the way through.

Transfer the chicken to a plate (reserve the stock to use in soups and sauces) and cool for 5 minutes, then shred the chicken into small pieces using two forks, going along the grain of the chicken. Cool completely and refrigerate as quickly as possible.

chicken with easy white sauce

- PREPARATION: 5 MINUTES
- COOKING: 10 MINUTES
- MAKES 2 PORTIONS
- PROVIDES PROTEIN, IRON, SELENIUM, CALCIUM, ZINC, FOLATE, VITS A, B_6, & D

75g (2½oz) shredded chicken with 150ml (5fl oz) of its stock (see above)

15g (½oz) butter

1 small shallot, diced

15g (½oz) plain flour

3 tbsp double cream

2 tbsp frozen peas

Melt the butter in a pan, add the shallot, and sauté for 5 minutes until softened. Stir in the flour and cook for 1 minute. Remove from the heat. Stir in the stock a little at a time to make a smooth sauce. Return to the heat and slowly bring to a simmer, stirring until thickened. Add the cream, peas, and shredded chicken. Simmer for 2 minutes until everything is hot. (Reheat leftovers in the microwave for about 2 minutes, stirring halfway through, until piping hot.) Allow to cool to warm before serving.

cheesy scrambled eggs

Well-cooked scrambled eggs are fine for your baby from around six months – egg allergies are less common than most people think. It's a pity not to give children eggs as they are so quick and easy to prepare and so nutritious. If you prefer, leave out the spring onion, and try using other types of cheese. Double the quantities for hungry children.

- PREPARATION: 5 MINUTES
- COOKING: 3–4 MINUTES
- MAKES 1 PORTION
- PROVIDES PROTEIN, CALCIUM, VITS C, D, & E, PREBIOTICS

1 egg

1½ tsp milk

Knob of butter

1 small spring onion, sliced

1 small tomato, skinned, deseeded, and chopped

Small handful of grated Cheddar cheese

Beat the egg with the milk. Melt the butter in a medium saucepan and, when foaming, add the spring onion and cook for 30 seconds. Add the eggs with the chopped tomato and cook gently, stirring, until scrambled. Remove from the heat, sprinkle over the cheese, and stir in until slightly melted.

creamy courgette rice

I tend to make this as a quick and easy side dish for griddled chicken. You could double the quantities and add 2 tsp freshly grated Parmesan if you want to make it a meal in itself.

- PREPARATION: 5 MINUTES
- COOKING: 6–8 MINUTES
- MAKES 1 PORTION
- PROVIDES CALCIUM, FOLATE, VITS A, B$_2$, & C

¼ medium courgette (50g/scant 2oz)

Small knob of butter

3 tbsp cooked rice

2 tbsp milk

Grate the courgette on the fine side of a box grater. Melt the butter in a saucepan, add the courgette, and cook gently for 5–6 minutes until the courgette is soft. Stir in the rice and milk. Bring up to a simmer and cook for 1–2 minutes until the rice is hot and the milk is almost completely absorbed. Cool slightly before serving.

date baby first tried ....

baby's reaction ....

what I thought ....

my variations ....

tick reaction

date baby first tried ....

baby's reaction ....

what I thought ....

my variations ....

tick reaction

finger-size salmon fishcakes

These fishcakes are crumbed so they aren't too squishy to survive being picked up, but for older children (who eat with forks), you could make tablespoon-sized cakes and just dust them in flour before frying. The ketchup in this recipe gives a subtle tang – add more if you like.

- PREPARATION: 25 MINUTES, PLUS OPTIONAL OVERNIGHT CHILLING
- COOKING: ABOUT 4 MINUTES
- MAKES 24–26 (4–6 PORTIONS)
- PROVIDES PROTEIN, OMEGA-3s, IRON, CALCIUM, VITS C, D, & E
- SUITABLE FOR FREEZING

I medium potato (about 250g/9oz)

1 recipe Perfectly poached salmon (page 100), or 150g (5½oz) store-bought poached salmon, skin removed

1 large or 2 small spring onions, finely chopped

1 tbsp mayonnaise

3–4 tsp tomato ketchup (to taste)

2 tbsp plain flour

1 egg, beaten

4 tbsp dried breadcrumbs

3 tbsp freshly grated Parmesan cheese

5–6 tbsp sunflower oil, for frying

Microwave the potato for 7–9 minutes (depending on wattage) until soft. Leave to stand for 10 minutes or until cool enough to handle, then peel off the skin with a sharp knife.

Put the potato in a bowl and mash well. Flake the salmon and stir into the potato together with the spring onions, mayonnaise, and ketchup. Mix well – you don't want any large pieces of salmon. Roll teaspoonfuls of the mixture into small balls.

Put the flour on a plate; put the egg in a bowl; mix the breadcrumbs and Parmesan together on another plate. Dust the balls with flour, then dip in egg and coat in breadcrumbs. For best results, cover and chill overnight.

Heat the oil in a frying pan and cook the fishcakes for about 4 minutes, turning occasionally, until golden brown on all sides. Drain on kitchen paper and allow to cool to warm before serving.

Note: To freeze, open freeze, then store in a freezer bag; cook from frozen, adding 1 minute to the cooking time.

date baby first tried ....

baby's reaction ....

what I thought ....

my variations ....

tick reaction

perfectly poached salmon

Try to give your baby omega-3-rich salmon or other oily fish twice a week. Salmon breaks into nice large flakes that are easy to eat.

- PREPARATION: 5 MINUTES
- COOKING: 10 MINUTES
- MAKES 2–3 PORTIONS
- PROVIDES PROTEIN, OMEGA-3s, IRON, SELENIUM, VITS A & E

500ml (17fl oz) vegetable or fish stock

150g (5½oz) piece of salmon fillet (skin on), about 2cm (¾in) thick

Put the stock in a medium-sized saucepan and bring up to a simmer. Add the salmon, flesh side down, and cook at a very gentle simmer for 7 minutes. Turn the salmon over and cook for a further 2–3 minutes until the fish is opaque all the way through and breaks into large flakes when pressed with a fork. (Thicker pieces of salmon may take a couple of minutes longer.)

Transfer the salmon to a plate and allow to cool slightly before peeling off the skin and scraping away any dark meat (this has a strong flavour that may be a bit much for babies). Break into large flakes to serve.

carrot and orange salad

Coarsely grated carrot is a useful early finger food as it has a familiar taste and is easy to swallow. You can add 1 tbsp raisins and a few sunflower seeds to make this a tasty salad for older children.

- PREPARATION: 5 MINUTES, PLUS AT LEAST 1 HOUR CHILLING
- COOKING: NONE
- MAKES 2–3 PORTIONS
- PROVIDES BETA-CAROTENE, VIT C

1 medium carrot, peeled and coarsely grated (50g/scant 2oz)

2 tsp orange juice

1 tsp olive oil

Salt and pepper

Mix the carrot, juice, and oil together and season with a little pepper (you can add salt for children over 12 months). Cover and chill for at least 1 hour, or overnight, before serving.

poached chicken balls

Traditionally cooked meatballs can be too chewy for first finger foods, but poaching makes them tender, perfect for little ones. The meatballs can be served alone, or with a tomato sauce for older children.

- PREPARATION: 25 MINUTES
- COOKING: 4–5 MINUTES
- MAKES ABOUT 20 (4–7 PORTIONS)
- PROVIDES PROTEIN, IRON, ZINC, CALCIUM, SELENIUM, FOLATE, VITS C & D
- SUITABLE FOR FREEZING

1 shallot, diced

1 tsp olive oil

110g (4oz) minced chicken

20g (¾oz) fresh breadcrumbs

¼ eating apple, peeled and coarsely grated

3 tbsp freshly grated Parmesan cheese

¼ tsp fresh thyme leaves

Pepper

750ml (1¼ pints) chicken stock

Sauté the shallot in the oil for 5–6 minutes until soft. Transfer to a food processor and leave to cool for 5 minutes. Add the chicken, breadcrumbs, apple, Parmesan, and thyme, and season with a little pepper. Whiz until well combined. Roll teaspoonfuls of the mixture into small balls.

Put the stock in a saucepan and bring to the boil. Add the chicken balls and poach gently for 4–5 minutes until cooked through. Remove with a slotted spoon and cool to warm (cut the balls in half for smaller babies).

Note: To reheat a single portion, put the chicken balls in a small bowl and add 1 tsp water. Cover and microwave on high for 30–40 seconds until piping hot. Do not overcook as they will turn rubbery. Allow to cool to warm.

date baby first tried ....

baby's reaction ....

what I thought ....

my variations ....

tick reaction

date baby first tried ....

baby's reaction ....

....

....

....

what I thought ....

....

....

my variations ....

....

....

....

....

....

tick
reaction

mini oat and raisin biscuits

There is something very comforting about the smell of home-baked biscuits wafting through the house. Oats are one of the most nutritious grains, and they help to stabilize blood sugar, giving long-lasting energy. These oat biscuits are very quick and easy to prepare, and are fun to make with older children.

- PREPARATION: 15 MINUTES
- COOKING: 10–12 MINUTES
- MAKES ABOUT 18
- PROVIDES IRON, VITS B_1, B_2, B_3, PREBIOTICS
- SUITABLE FOR FREEZING

85g (3oz) soft butter

75g (2½oz) soft light brown sugar

2 tsp golden syrup

1 tsp pure vanilla extract

50g (scant 2oz) plain flour

¼ tsp bicarbonate of soda

Pinch of salt
(not for babies under 1 year)

75g (2½oz) rolled oats

55g (2oz) raisins, cut in half

Preheat the oven to 180°C (160°C fan), gas 4.
    Cream the butter, sugar, and golden syrup together until pale and fluffy, then beat in the vanilla extract. Fold in the flour, bicarbonate of soda, salt, and oats, followed by the halved raisins. Form into about 18 small balls and arrange on baking trays lined with baking parchment.
    Bake for 10–12 minutes, rotating the baking trays halfway through if you are not using a fan oven. Leave to cool on the trays for a few minutes before transferring to a wire rack. The biscuits will crisp up as they cool.

meal planner: fingers and spoons

This meal planner provides suggestions for your baby's meals, many of which are drawn from this book. Either use the planner pages to map out your baby's meals for the next weeks or to keep a record of your baby's diet week-by-week.

breakfast	lunch	dinner	extras
My first muesli (p88) fruit	Chicken with easy white sauce (p96) fruit	Tomato, sweet potato, and cheese sauce with pasta shells (pp94–95)	Finger food sandwiches (pp90–92) fruit
scrambled egg and toast fruit	Finger-size salmon fishcakes (pp98–99) with peas yogurt	My favourite chicken purée (p72)	rice cakes fruit
French toast fingers (p89) Apple and pear purée (p58)	Broccoli and cheese baby bites (p93) fruit	My first beef casserole (p71) steamed broccoli and carrot	Mini oat and raisin biscuits (pp102–103) fruit
Porridge with apple, pear, and apricot (p70) yogurt	Poached chicken balls (p101) Iced banana smoothie stick (p136)	Fillet of fish with cheesy vegetable sauce (pp74–75)	Finger food sandwiches (pp90–92) fruit
cereal Apple and pear purée (p58)	Cheesy scrambled eggs (p97) and toast fingers yogurt	Chicken with easy white sauce (p96) and Creamy courgette rice (p97) fruit	dried apricots rice cakes
grilled cheese on toast mango or peach	Tomato, sweet potato, and cheese pasta (pp94–95) Strawberry milkshake ice lolly (p136)	My favourite chicken purée (p72) with Baked sweet potato purée (p57) fruit	toast fingers with peanut butter vegetable sticks
French toast fingers (p89) yogurt	grilled lamb chops, cut into strips with steamed carrot and cauliflower fruit	Tasty vegetable trio (p68) Iced banana smoothie stick (p136) fruit	Finger food sandwiches (pp90–92) fruit

● healthy breakfasts

Baby porridge oats provide a great base for introducing new tastes to your baby. Add your baby's favourite fruit purée or mashed fruit for a nutritious breakfast.

WEEK 1	breakfast	lunch	dinner	extras
day 1				
day 2				
day 3				
day 4				
day 5				
day 6				
day 7				

meal planner: weeks 2 and 3

Use these planners to record the meals you give your baby over the following weeks. If you want to record your baby's meals for longer than three weeks, simply photocopy this page. Give your baby pieces of fruit or yogurt as snacks or desserts.

WEEK 2	breakfast	lunch	dinner	extras
day 1				
day 2				
day 3				
day 4				
day 5				
day 6				
day 7				

● lumpier food

Soft pasta shells are great first foods when you're introducing texture and lumpiness to your baby's food. Cold, cooked pasta shapes are good energy-boosting snacks too.

WEEK 3	breakfast	lunch	dinner	extras
day 1				
day 2				
day 3				
day 4				
day 5				
day 6				
day 7				

other favourites

Use this page to note down your other favourite recipes, ideas for snacks and finger foods, good recipes for introducing lumpier foods to your baby, or recipe recommendations from your friends and family. Enjoy experimenting!

toddlers: 12–18 months

"Running around after an energetic toddler can be hard work, so here are some simple but delicious meals and healthy snacks that are quick and easy to prepare."

energy boosters

Toddlers are on the go all the time, whether they're crawling or taking their first uneasy steps, so it's important to keep their energy levels up and provide them with healthy meals and energy-boosling snacks.

Your child's increased independence means that she may become reluctant to sit at the table, so you will need to adapt to her changing needs. This is also a time when your toddler will have much more interaction with other children – at nursery or playgroups, for example – and is likely to pick up bugs. Healthy, nutrient-packed foods can make all the difference in keeping illnesses at bay and boosting your little one's immunity.

● eating as a family

At 12 months your child can eat most foods and should be enjoying a full and varied diet. You'll find it will become much easier to include her in family meals. It is important to try to eat together whenever possible as children are more likely to eat if they see you eating too. It's also a good opportunity for your child to try new foods. Many of the recipes in this section are suitable for the whole family too, such as Chicken parmigiana (pages 124–125), Hidden vegetable bolognaise (pages 126–127), Orchard crumble (page 130), and First fruit fool (pages 132–133).

Remember your child still needs to avoid whole nuts, unpasteurized cheese, very salty or spicy foods, and highly refined sugary foods.

● energy-boosting foods

Meals and snacks that give your active toddler a steady stream of energy are vital. Carbohydrates that release sugars slowly into the bloodstream are best. The best sources are rice, potatoes,

a vegetarian diet

✱ **A balanced vegetarian diet** can be very healthy, but it is important to provide the nutrients that meat provides, particularly iron.

✱ **Non-meat sources of iron** include all pulses, fortified wholegrain cereals, and leafy green vegetables, but the iron in these foods is not so readily absorbed as that in red meat.

✱ **Combine these foods** with vitamin C-rich foods or drinks to help absorb the iron, for example orange juice with breakfast cereal.

✱ **A good vegetarian diet for a child** should include cheese and eggs. Adult vegetarian diets containing bulky foods like wholegrains, lentils, and brown rice are unsuitable for children under the age of two as their tummies will be full before they get all the nutrients they need.

pasta, and wholegrain cereals. They provide long-lasting energy and avoid sudden highs and lows in blood sugar, which can cause mood swings and poor concentration.

● healthy snacks

Your toddler's tummy is only little, so don't overload her plate at mealtimes and offer "top-up" snacks when she is hungry again.

Remember that snacks must be nutritious, and not simply quick ways to fill your child's tummy. Dried and fresh fruit, bread sticks, cheese, lean meats, boiled eggs, raw vegetables, yogurt, seeds, toast with nut butter, hummus, rice cakes, and mini muffins (try the bomb muffins on pages 116–117) are all healthy options and will keep your baby's energy levels up between meals. It's a good idea to have a supply of easy-to-prepare, nutritious snacks to hand, so you aren't tempted to resort to biscuits and chocolate.

High-sugar snacks, like biscuits, cakes, sugary cereals, and soft drinks, cause a rapid rise in blood sugar. They are perfectly acceptable in small amounts, after or as part of a balanced meal, but when given alone, the body overcompensates for the rapid rise in blood sugar and produces large amounts of insulin, which then causes a dip in blood sugar levels.

● drinks

While it's best to give your child water, a little diluted orange juice at mealtimes will help with iron absorption (especially if she is vegetarian – see box, page 111, for more on this). Always dilute fruit juice (at least three parts water to one part juice), and give juice only at mealtimes.

Children are at greater risk of tooth decay than adults because their newly formed teeth are more vulnerable to acid, so give juice to your child only in a cup or beaker and try to do away with bottles

food for the brain

My child is dyspraxic and I've been told that including oily fish in his diet can help. How can I encourage him to eat fish?

It's true that oil-rich fish such as salmon is good for the brain, due to the high level of omega-3 fatty acids. There is overwhelming evidence that increasing the intake of essential fatty acids from oily fish can result in improved concentration, learning, and behaviour, and it has been shown to revolutionize the lives of kids with dyslexia, ADHD, and dyspraxia. It's important not to put children off eating fish as it's such a great food. Overcooked fish is dry and tasteless (it needs just a few minutes in a pan or microwave). Be sure to remove all bones. Small portions are attractive to kids – try making mini fish pies (page 120) and salmon fishcakes (page 99).

ask annabel

tips

By 12 months try to do away with the bottle and move your baby to a cup or beaker

Broccoli is a true superfood. It's a good source of vitamin C and is packed with nutrients that help prevent illness

Fresh fruit ice lollies are a great way to give more fluids to your baby when she is feeling unwell

by the time your baby is one; perhaps reserve a bottle of milk for bedtime only. Sweet drinks at bedtime, once the teeth are brushed, are not a good idea as there is not enough saliva in the mouth to wash away harmful acid.

● feeding a poorly child

Fluid intake is the main priority over food, so make sure you offer your child drinks at frequent intervals. A good way to give more fluids is to make fresh fruit ice lollies for your child to suck (see recipe on pages 135–137).

If your child has been feverish, try to bring her temperature down before a mealtime. She is extremely unlikely to eat much if she has a high temperature, and is more likely to vomit. If your child refuses the food or becomes distressed, remove the food immediately, trying not to let your stress or disappointment show. Replace the time you would have been feeding your child with a good cuddle or perhaps a massage.

> "Your toddler's tummy is only little, so don't overload her plate at mealtimes and offer "top-up" snacks when she is hungry again"

When children are unwell they often lose their appetite, which can be worrying for parents. Parents seem to have a natural instinct to try to feed their children no matter what, but the fact of the matter is that for a few days children can survive perfectly well on a minuscule amount of food. Their growth rate may slow down or they may even lose a little weight during an illness, but children who are otherwise healthy should make up for this when they feel better.

As your child's appetite returns, offer simple meals and healthy snacks at usual times. Be sure to include energy-boosting, slow-releasing carbohydrates in meals, such as wholegrain cereals, pasta, potatoes, and fruit and vegetables, as you may find that your child is still exhausted days after her other symptoms have disappeared. See "foods to fight illness" (on the following page). Keep things simple, though – after all, this is not the ideal time for you to spend hours in the supermarket or kitchen, experimenting with a new recipe.

If your toddler has been prescribed antibiotics, it's a good idea to give her some live yogurt. Antibiotics kill off the bad and good bacteria in the intestine, but giving your child live yogurt will help to replace the good bacteria.

foods to fight illness

✴ Garlic contains allicin, which is a natural antibiotic, antiviral, and antifungal agent.

✴ Vitamin C-rich foods boost the body's levels of vitamin C, which are depleted during illness, and are thought to reduce cold symptoms. Vitamin C is also needed for the healing of wounds. Good sources include kiwi fruit, citrus fruits, sweet peppers, blackcurrants, dark green leafy vegetables, and strawberries.

✴ Apple is very easy to digest. In the US, the BRAT diet (bananas, rice, apples, and toast) is often suggested by doctors for the relief of diarrhoea. Pectin, the soluble fibre contained in apples, also helps to relieve constipation. Make sure the apples are peeled.

✴ Bananas are packed full of slow-release sugars for sustained energy. They are also great for diarrhoea because they help to bulk the stool. However, they do seem to cause constipation in some susceptible babies.

nutrients to prevent illness

✴ Vitamin A, found in liver, oily fish, milk, cheese, butter, and egg yolks, can help prevent infection of the nose, throat, and lungs.

✴ Beta-carotene boosts the immune system against colds and flu. Orange and yellow fruits and vegetables contain high levels. These include carrots, butternut squash, sweet potatoes, swedes, cantaloupe melons, and apricots.

✴ Essential fatty acids found in salmon and other oily fish support brain function and the immune system. Try to give your child oily fish twice a week.

✴ Iron, found in red meats, liver, dried fruits, and iron-enriched cereals, is needed to prevent iron-deficiency anaemia. This, sadly, is a common condition that is usually preventable, and it makes children more susceptible to frequent infections.

tummy troubles

If your baby hasn't done a poo for more than three days, or her poo is so hard that it causes discomfort, you need to make sure that she drinks plenty of juice, especially prune juice, and water, and include lots of fruit and vegetables in her diet. Give her high-fibre cereals, such as porridge, and avoid too much rice, banana, and stodgy food, such as macaroni cheese, as these can be binding.

goujons of fish

I like to serve these deliciously crisp goujons with a little tomato ketchup or tartare sauce for dipping.

- PREPARATION: 15–20 MINUTES
- COOKING: 2–3 MINUTES
- MAKES ABOUT 16 (3–4 PORTIONS)
- PROVIDES PROTEIN, IRON, CALCIUM, SELENIUM, VITS B$_6$ & C
- SUITABLE FOR FREEZING

170g (6oz) skinless lemon sole fillets (or similar white fish fillets)

2 tbsp plain flour

55g (2oz) panko breadcrumbs (or ordinary dried breadcrumbs)

30g (1oz) Parmesan cheese, freshly grated

Finely grated zest of ¼ lemon

Large pinch of paprika (or to taste)

Salt and pepper

1 egg, beaten with a pinch of salt

4–5 tbsp sunflower oil, for frying

Pat the fish dry with kitchen paper and cut into pieces the size of a little finger. Spread out the flour on a large plate. Mix the crumbs, Parmesan cheese, and lemon zest together on another large plate and season with the paprika and some salt and pepper. Crack the egg into a small bowl and whisk well.

Toss the fish goujons in the flour and shake off any excess, then dip in the egg and, finally, roll in the crumb mixture.

Heat the oil in a large frying pan or wok over a medium heat and fry the goujons for 1–1½ minutes on each side until golden and the fish is cooked. Drain on kitchen paper and allow to cool to warm before serving.

Note: To freeze, open freeze, then transfer to bags; fry from frozen, allowing 30 seconds extra cooking time.

date baby first tried ....

baby's reaction ....
....
....
....

what I thought ....
....
....

my variations ....
....
....
....
....

tick reaction

date baby first tried ....

baby's reaction ....

what I thought ....

my variations ....

tick reaction

bomb muffins (banana, oat, maple, and blueberry)

If your baby dislikes too much texture, put the ingredients for the muffin mixture in a food processor and whiz them together, then add the blueberries and pulse three or four times to chop.

- PREPARATION: 15–20 MINUTES
- COOKING: 12–14 MINUTES
- MAKES 24 MINI OR 6 LARGE
- PROVIDES POTASSIUM, VITS A, B_3, & C, PREBIOTICS
- SUITABLE FOR FREEZING

30g (1oz) rolled oats

85g (3oz) plain wholemeal flour

½ tsp bicarbonate of soda

½ tsp baking powder

½ tsp ground cinnamon

½ tsp ground ginger

¼ tsp salt

1 very ripe banana, mashed

1 egg

30g (1oz) butter, melted

4 tbsp maple syrup

3 tbsp soft light brown sugar

¾ tsp pure vanilla extract

55g (2oz) blueberries

1 tbsp demerara or maple sugar

Preheat the oven to 180°C (160°C fan), gas 4. Line two mini muffin tins (each with 12 cups) with paper cases.

In a large bowl mix together the oats, flour, bicarbonate of soda, baking powder, cinnamon, ginger, and salt. In a separate bowl mix together the banana, egg, butter, syrup, brown sugar, and vanilla extract. Mix the wet ingredients into the dry until just combined, then fold in the blueberries.

Spoon into the muffin cases, filling them three-quarters full. Sprinkle a little demerara sugar on each muffin. Bake for 12–14 minutes until risen and firm to the touch. Cool on a wire rack.

Note: If frozen, remove the muffins as needed and thaw for 30 minutes at room temperature.

Variation: If you don't have mini muffin tins, you can make six regular-size muffins, which will take 15–17 minutes to bake. Cut the muffins into cubes or small pieces for toddlers.

> Just one serving of blueberries provides as many disease-fighting antioxidants as five servings of carrots, apples, squash, or broccoli

date baby first tried ....

baby's reaction ....

....

....

what I thought ....

....

my variations ....

....

....

tick
reaction

baked pita crisps

These are handy for snacks – and heathier than potato crisps. Store them in an airtight tin or box. The Cinnamon-sugar pita crisps are nice dipped into yogurt.

parmesan and herb pita crisps

- PREPARATION: 10 MINUTES
- COOKING: 8–10 MINUTES
- MAKES 16
- PROVIDES CALCIUM, VITS B_1 & B_3

2 small (or 1 large) wholemeal or plain pita breads

1 tbsp olive oil, plus extra for greasing

3 tbsp freshly grated Parmesan cheese

½ tsp chopped fresh thyme (optional)

Preheat the oven to 180°C (160°C fan), gas 4.

Cut the pitas into quarters (cut large pitas into eighths) and peel the pieces apart to give 16 triangles. Brush both sides of each triangle with olive oil (you may not need all of the oil) and set, smooth side down, on an oiled baking tray. Sprinkle over the Parmesan and thyme (if using). Bake for 8–10 minutes, watching carefully after the first 6 minutes to be sure the crisps do not brown too much. Cool on a wire rack.

date baby first tried ....

baby's reaction ....

....

....

....

....

what I thought ....

....

my variations ....

....

....

....

tick
reaction

cinnamon-sugar pita crisps

- PREPARATION: 10–15 MINUTES
- COOKING: ABOUT 20 MINUTES
- MAKES 16
- PROVIDES VITS A, B_1, & B_3

2 small (or 1 large) wholemeal or plain pita breads

30g (1oz) butter

2 tsp soft light brown sugar

½ tsp ground cinnamon

Preheat the oven to 130°C (110°C fan), gas 1.

Cut the pitas into quarters (cut large pitas into eighths) and peel the pieces apart to give 16 triangles. Put the butter, sugar, and cinnamon in a small saucepan and stir over a low heat until melted. Brush both sides of the pita triangles generously with the butter mixture (you may not need all of it) and set on a baking tray lined with baking parchment. Bake for 10 minutes, then turn the crisps over and bake for a further 9–10 minutes. Cool on a wire rack – they will crisp up as they cool.

tuna tortilla melt

Tuna is a true superfood standby, rich in protein and vitamins
(I prefer tuna packed in oil rather than brine). The good thing about a
tortilla sandwich is that it is nice and thin, perfect for little ones.

- PREPARATION: 5 MINUTES
- COOKING: 2–4 MINUTES
- MAKES 1 LARGE PORTION
- PROVIDES PROTEIN, CALCIUM, IRON,
  SELENIUM, VITS A, C, & D

½ x 185g (6½oz) tin tuna, drained

1 tbsp crème fraîche or soured cream

2 tsp tomato ketchup

2–3 drops of lemon juice

1 spring onion, finely chopped

30g (1oz) Cheddar cheese, grated

1 small flour tortilla wrap

If using the grill to cook the sandwich, preheat it. Mix the tuna, crème
fraîche, ketchup, lemon juice, and spring onion together. Stir in the Cheddar.
Spread the mixture over half of the tortilla, then fold the other half over to
sandwich in the filling. Grill, or toast in a dry frying pan, for 1–2 minutes on
each side until crisp and browned. Cool to warm before cutting into fingers.

toasted peanut butter and banana sandwich

Protein-rich peanut butter and banana make a very dynamic duo! I like
to roll out the bread so that the sandwich is a little thinner and easier
to eat. Make half a sandwich if your child has a small appetite.

- PREPARATION: 5 MINUTES
- COOKING: ABOUT 4 MINUTES
- MAKES 1 LARGE PORTION
- PROVIDES PROTEIN, MAGNESIUM,
  POTASSIUM, VITS A, B_1, B_3, & E

1 rounded tbsp smooth peanut butter

2 slices bread, flattened

½ small banana, mashed

15g (½oz) soft butter

Preheat the grill to high. Spread the peanut butter over the bread, then
spread the banana on top of one slice and sandwich together. Spread the
butter in a thin layer over the outside of both sides of the sandwich, going
right to the edges. Grill for about 2 minutes on each side until crisp and
golden. Cool to warm, then cut into fingers using a serrated knife.

date baby first tried..........

baby's reaction ....
....
....

what I thought ....
....
....

my variations ....
....
....

tick reaction

date baby first tried..........

baby's reaction ....
....
....

what I thought ....
....
....

my variations ....
....
....

tick reaction

date baby first tried ....

baby's reaction ....
....
....
....
....

what I thought ....
....
....
....
....

my variations ....
....
....
....
....
....

tick
reaction

first fish pie

I like to keep cubes of puréed squash in the freezer as a standby vegetable and they are also useful for adding to sauces. To make the purée from scratch, you need to steam 90g (generous 3oz) peeled and cubed butternut squash for 8–10 minutes until soft, then mash or whiz in a blender or food processor.

- PREPARATION: 30 MINUTES
- COOKING: 20–25 MINUTES
- MAKES 4–6 INDIVIDUAL PIES
- PROVIDES PROTEIN, CALCIUM, SELENIUM, IRON, BETA-CAROTENE, VITS A, C, D, & E
- SUITABLE FOR FREEZING

250g (9oz) skinless cod fillet (or similar white fish), cubed

Topping

500g (1lb 2oz) potatoes, peeled and cubed

15g (½oz) butter

3 tbsp milk

Salt and pepper

Sauce

10g (⅓oz) butter

10g (⅓oz) plain flour

150ml (5fl oz) milk

80g (scant 3oz) butternut squash purée (see above)

55g (2oz) mature Cheddar cheese, grated

2 tbsp freshly grated Parmesan cheese

Divide the cubed fish among four to six small ovenproof dishes or ramekins.

Cook the potatoes in plenty of boiling salted water for about 15 minutes until just tender. Drain the potatoes, then mash well. Beat in the butter and milk, and season to taste with salt and pepper.

Make the sauce while the potatoes are cooking. Melt the butter in a small saucepan, then stir in the flour and cook for 1 minute. Remove from the heat and gradually stir in the milk until you have a smooth sauce. Return to a low heat and cook, stirring constantly, until the sauce comes to the boil and thickens. Stir in the squash purée, then remove from the heat and stir in the cheeses until melted. Cool slightly before spooning over the fish.

Preheat the oven to 200°C (180°C fan), gas 6. Spoon the mashed potatoes over the fish and sauce, and mark the surface with ridges using a fork.

Set the dish(es) on a baking tray and bake for 20 minutes until hot in the centre and golden on top. If the pies are fridge-cold, bake them for an extra 5 minutes. The tops can be browned further under a hot grill, if you like.

Note: To freeze, wrap the potato-topped pies well; thaw overnight in the fridge before baking.

date baby first tried ....

baby's reaction ....

....

....

....

....

what I thought ....

....

....

my variations ....

....

....

....

....

....

....

tick
reaction

cheese and peas orzo

Orzo, which is small rice-shaped pasta, is easy to swallow and good for smaller children (use stelline or other small pasta shapes if you cannot get orzo). This dish is quite "sticky" when cooked, so is useful for toddlers who are trying to use a spoon or fork – there's a good chance some will stay on the utensil and reach the mouth!

- PREPARATION: 5 MINUTES
- COOKING: 12–15 MINUTES
- MAKES 1 PORTION
- PROVIDES PROTEIN, POTASSIUM,
  CALCIUM, FOLATE, VITS A, C, & D

2 tbsp orzo

1 tbsp frozen peas (petits pois if possible)

1 tbsp crème fraîche or double cream

20g (¾oz) Cheddar cheese, finely grated

1 tsp freshly grated Parmesan cheese

Cook the orzo according to packet instructions (you can use vegetable stock instead of water for more flavour). Add the peas for the final minute of cooking. Drain well and return the orzo and peas to the saucepan over a low heat.

Stir in the crème fraîche and bubble for a couple of minutes until almost fully absorbed. Remove from the heat and stir in the Cheddar until melted. Cool slightly to warm before serving with the Parmesan.

quick chicken risotto

If you are in a real hurry then you can omit the shallot and broccoli and just add 1 tbsp peas with the chicken.

- PREPARATION: 5–10 MINUTES
- COOKING: 8–10 MINUTES
- MAKES 1 PORTION
- PROVIDES PROTEIN, IRON, ZINC, FOLATE, SELENIUM, VITS A, B$_3$, B$_{12}$, C, & D

1 tsp butter

1 tsp finely diced shallot

45g (1½oz) small broccoli florets

55g (2oz) cooked rice

4 tbsp chicken stock

30g (1oz) cooked chicken, shredded (see page 96)

1 tbsp freshly grated Parmesan cheese

Melt the butter in a small saucepan and sauté the shallot for 5–6 minutes until soft. Meanwhile, steam the broccoli for 3–4 minutes until just tender.

Add the rice, stock, chicken, and cooked broccoli to the saucepan and simmer for 2–3 minutes until most of the stock has been absorbed. Remove from the heat and stir in the Parmesan.

pasta with simple squash and cheese sauce

If you keep cubes of butternut squash or pumpkin purée in the freezer, you can thaw one and whip up this sauce in no time (see page 56 for how to make the purée from scratch). You could add a splash of double cream, if you have any in the fridge.

- PREPARATION: 5 MINUTES
- COOKING: 10–12 MINUTES
- MAKES 1 PORTION
- PROVIDES PROTEIN, CALCIUM, BETA-CAROTENE, VITS A, D, & E

30g (1oz) small pasta shapes or macaroni

2 tbsp butternut squash purée (see above)

2 tbsp milk

30g (1oz) Gruyère or Cheddar cheese, finely grated

Salt and pepper

Cook the pasta according to the packet instructions. Drain and return to the pan over a low heat. Add the squash purée and milk, and stir until hot. Remove from the heat and stir in the cheese until melted. Season to taste.

date baby first tried ....

baby's reaction ....

what I thought ....

my variations ....

tick reaction

date baby first tried ....

baby's reaction ....

what I thought ....

my variations ....

tick reaction

date baby first tried ....

baby's reaction ....

....

....

....

what I thought ....

....

....

my variations ....

....

....

....

....

....

tick
reaction

chicken parmigiana

I would defy even the fussiest child to reject this dish as it ticks all of the right boxes for baby tastebuds – crumb-coated chicken, tomato sauce, and melted cheese. It is a great dish to grow up with – just cut the cooked chicken into pieces suitable for your child's age and teeth.

- PREPARATION: 10–15 MINUTES
- COOKING: 30 MINUTES
- MAKES 4 PORTIONS
- PROVIDES PROTEIN, IRON, SELENIUM, ZINC, CALCIUM, VITS C, D, & E, PREBIOTICS
- SUITABLE FOR FREEZING

1 large shallot, diced

1 tbsp olive oil

1 small clove garlic, crushed

1 x 400g (14oz) tin chopped tomatoes

1½ tbsp tomato purée

1 tsp sugar

Salt and pepper

2 x 140g (5oz) skinless, boneless chicken breasts

1 egg, beaten

2 tbsp plain flour

55g (2oz) dried breadcrumbs

3–4 tbsp sunflower oil, for frying

55g (2oz) mozzarella cheese, grated

2 tbsp freshly grated Parmesan cheese

Put the shallot and olive oil in a wok or large pan and sauté for 4–5 minutes until soft. Add the garlic and cook for 1 minute, then stir in the tomatoes, tomato purée, and sugar. Simmer for 20–25 minutes until thick. Season to taste. Remove from the heat and blend to a purée. Keep warm.

While the sauce is simmering, cut the chicken breasts in half horizontally and lay each half out flat. Cover with cling film and beat out until about 5mm (¼in) thick. Put the egg in a bowl; spread the flour on a large plate; spread the breadcrumbs on a second large plate and season them. Dust the flattened chicken breast halves with flour, then dip in the egg, and, finally, coat with the breadcrumbs.

Heat the sunflower oil in a large non-stick frying pan and cook the chicken breasts over a medium heat for about 3 minutes on each side until the coating is golden brown and the chicken is just cooked. Drain briefly on kitchen paper and transfer to an ovenproof dish. Preheat the grill to high.

Spread about 3 tbsp of tomato sauce over each chicken breast and scatter over the mozzarella and Parmesan. Grill for 3–4 minutes until the cheese is bubbling. Cool slightly before serving.

Note: Freeze the sauce and coated chicken separately. Fry the chicken from frozen, adding an extra 1–2 minutes per side to the cooking time; reheat the sauce and complete the recipe.

hidden vegetable bolognaise

If your child won't eat vegetables, then bolognaise is a good way to hide them. The apple is an unusual ingredient but adds a sweetness that children enjoy. Serve with spaghetti or other pasta, or with rice.

- PREPARATION: 15 MINUTES
- COOKING: 1 HOUR
- MAKES 8 PORTIONS
- PROVIDES PROTEIN, IRON, SELENIUM, ZINC, BETA-CAROTENE, FOLATE, VITS B$_2$, B$_3$ & C, PREBIOTICS
- SUITABLE FOR FREEZING

1 tbsp olive oil

1 small onion, finely chopped

1 small leek, thinly sliced

½ stick celery, diced

¼ small red pepper, diced

1 small carrot, peeled and grated

½ eating apple, peeled and grated

1 clove garlic, crushed

1 x 400g (14oz) tin chopped tomatoes

450g (1lb) minced beef

4 tbsp tomato purée

2 tbsp tomato ketchup

250ml (9fl oz) beef stock

¼ tsp dried oregano

Salt and pepper

Heat the oil in a large frying pan and sauté the vegetables, apple, and garlic for 10 minutes until soft. Transfer to a blender and add the tomatoes, then whiz until smooth.

Wipe out the pan with a piece of kitchen paper, then add the mince and fry over a medium-high heat, breaking the mince up with a wooden spoon, until browned (you may need to do this in two batches). If your child likes a finer texture, you can transfer the browned mince to a food processor and whiz until well chopped.

Add the tomato and vegetable sauce to the mince and stir in the tomato purée, ketchup, stock, and oregano. Bring up to a simmer and cook for 40–45 minutes until the sauce is thick. Season to taste with salt and pepper.

date baby first tried ....

baby's reaction ....

....

....

....

what I thought ....

....

....

my variations ....

....

....

....

....

tick reaction

" This sauce is so versatile. Try mixing it with fusilli, top with béchamel sauce, sprinkle with grated cheese, and brown under the grill "

date baby first tried ....

....

baby's reaction ....

....

....

....

....

what I thought ....

....

....

....

my variations ....

....

....

....

....

....

....

tick
reaction

crunchy tofu cubes

Tofu is a good source of protein and its fairly soft texture makes it a good food for babies with few teeth. Vegans can omit the flour and egg part of the coating and just roll the marinated tofu cubes in breadcrumbs. However, you will need to cook the crumbed tofu immediately as the crumbs will go soggy if left standing. Also, the cubes will be a bit softer and less easy to pick up than the egg and breadcrumbed version. Note that this recipe is for toddlers over one year – salt in soy sauce is unsuitable for younger children.

- PREPARATION: 15–20 MINUTES, PLUS MINIMUM 8 HOURS MARINATING
- COOKING: 6 MINUTES
- MAKES 16
- PROVIDES PROTEIN, CALCIUM, VITS D & E

250g (9oz) extra firm tofu, cut into 2cm (¾in) cubes

½ tsp grated fresh root ginger

2 tsp soy sauce

1 tsp mirin

1 tsp clear honey

2 tbsp plain flour

1 egg, lightly beaten

30g (1oz) dried breadcrumbs (preferably honey panko)

5 tbsp sunflower oil, for frying

Blot as much excess liquid as possible from the tofu cubes, using kitchen paper. Mix the ginger, soy sauce, mirin, and honey together in a bowl. Add the tofu and toss to coat, then cover and marinate in the fridge for 8 hours, or overnight, turning the cubes once or twice.

Put the flour and egg in separate bowls and spread the breadcrumbs on a large plate. Remove the tofu cubes from the marinade, then dust with flour, dip in egg, and roll in breadcrumbs.

Put a thin layer of oil in a large non-stick frying pan and heat until shimmering. Drop a couple of breadcrumbs into the oil – if they sizzle straight away, the oil is hot enough. Fry the tofu cubes for 30–40 seconds on each side until golden brown all over. Drain on kitchen paper and allow to cool until warm before serving. Or serve cold.

ginger biscuit shapes

It is fun to use various novelty cutters, such as stars, circles, and flowers, so that your baby can learn the names of the shapes.

- PREPARATION: 25–30 MINUTES, PLUS 1–2 HOURS CHILLING
- COOKING: ABOUT 9 MINUTES
- MAKES ABOUT 30
- PROVIDES VITS A & E

45g (1½oz) butter, softened

70g (2½oz) soft light brown sugar

4 tbsp golden syrup

1 large egg yolk

170g (6oz) plain flour

2 tsp ground ginger

½ tsp bicarbonate of soda

¼ tsp salt

Beat the butter and sugar together until pale and fluffy, then beat in the golden syrup and egg yolk until just combined. Sift over the flour, ginger, bicarbonate of soda, and salt, and stir in with a wooden spoon to form a dough. Put the dough on a piece of cling film and pat into a disc about 1cm (½in) thick. Wrap up and refrigerate for 1–2 hours until firm.

Preheat the oven to 180°C (160°C fan), gas 4. Roll out the dough between two pieces of baking parchment until about 3mm (⅛in) thick. Cut out shapes that are about 4cm (1⅝in) in diameter, and use a palette knife to transfer them to baking trays lined with parchment. If the dough becomes too soft, then lift it, still on the parchment, on to a baking tray and pop in the freezer for 5–10 minutes to firm up.

Bake the biscuits for about 9 minutes until puffed and just turning golden around the edges. For crisper biscuits, bake for a further 2 minutes. Allow the biscuits to cool on the baking tray for 5 minutes, then transfer to a wire rack to cool completely. Store in an airtight tin.

date baby first tried ....

baby's reaction ....

....

....

....

what I thought ....

....

....

my variations ....

....

....

....

....

....

tick reaction

orchard crumble

These easy individual crumbles are very popular. To vary them, use smaller apples and pears and throw in a few blackberries for the last 2 minutes when cooking the fruit.

- PREPARATION: 15–20 MINUTES
- COOKING: 20–25 MINUTES
- MAKES 4 PORTIONS
- PROVIDES FOLATE, VITS A & C
- SUITABLE FOR FREEZING

2 large eating apples (e.g. Pink Lady or Golden Delicious), peeled, cored, and diced

2 large pears (e.g. Conference), peeled, cored, and diced

85g (3oz) plain flour

45g (1½oz) butter, cut into cubes

45g (1½oz) demerara sugar

¾ tsp ground cinnamon

¼ tsp salt

4 tsp granulated sugar, or to taste

Preheat the oven to 200°C (180°C fan), gas 6.

Put the fruit in a small saucepan and cook gently for 10–15 minutes until soft but not mushy. Meanwhile, put the flour in a bowl and rub in the butter until it looks like crumbs. Stir in the demerara sugar, cinnamon, and salt.

Remove the fruit from the heat and stir in the granulated sugar, adding more if the fruit isn't sweet enough. Divide the fruit among four ramekins (about 9cm/3¾in diameter) and sprinkle over the crumble topping. Bake for 20–25 minutes. Cool to warm before serving, with custard or ice cream.

Note: To freeze, cool the baked crumbles and wrap well; thaw overnight in the fridge, then reheat in the microwave for 1–2 minutes.

bananas "foster"

Who can resist bananas in a warm caramel sauce? Remember that hot sugar can take a while to cool down, so please be sure to check the temperature of the sauce before serving to small children.

- PREPARATION: 5 MINUTES
- COOKING: 2 MINUTES
- MAKES 2 PORTIONS
- PROVIDES POTASSIUM, VIT A (PLUS VIT D AND CALCIUM IF SERVED WITH ICE CREAM)

1 large, slightly under-ripe banana

15g (½ oz) butter

1 tbsp maple syrup

1 tbsp soft brown sugar

Pinch of ground cinnamon (optional)

Peel the banana and cut it in half crossways, then in half again lengthways. Put the butter, syrup, sugar, and cinnamon in a small non-stick frying pan. Melt over a low heat. Stir well, then increase the heat to medium. When the syrup is boiling, add the banana pieces, cut side down. Cook for 1 minute, then carefully turn the pieces over and cook for a further minute.

Lift the bananas into serving bowls and spoon over the sauce. Allow to cool to warm before serving with vanilla ice cream. (The bananas can be kept in the fridge for 24 hours; reheat in the microwave for 1 minute.)

coconut rice pudding

You can serve this warm or chilled – I prefer it chilled. The rice tends to set as it chills so you need to add some cream to soften it up.

- PREPARATION: 10 MINUTES
- COOKING: 20 MINUTES
- MAKES 3–4 PORTIONS
- PROVIDES VITS A, D, & E (PLUS ADDITIONAL VITS DEPENDING ON FRUIT PURÉE USED)

55g (2oz) jasmine rice

200ml (7fl oz) full-fat milk

200ml (7fl oz) coconut milk

1–2 tsp sugar (to taste)

2–3 drops of pure vanilla extract

To serve cold

5 tbsp whipping cream

3 tbsp mango or other fruit purée

Put the rice, milk, and coconut milk into a medium saucepan. Bring to the boil, then simmer, stirring occasionally, for 20 minutes until the rice is tender. Remove from the heat and stir in the sugar and vanilla extract.

If serving cold, stir 1 tbsp of the cream into the chilled rice to loosen it. Whip the remaining cream and fold in. Swirl mango purée over the top.

date baby first tried ....

baby's reaction ....

what I thought ....

my variations ....

tick reaction

date baby first tried ....

baby's reaction ....

what I thought ....

my variations ....

tick reaction

date baby first tried ....

baby's reaction ....

....

....

....

....

what I thought ....

....

....

my variations ....

....

....

....

....

....

tick
reaction

first fruit fool

Even fussy babies usually like a combination of sweet fruit mixed with creamy yogurt. Adults love this too, so you may need to make double!

- PREPARATION: 10 MINUTES
- COOKING: NONE
- MAKES 4 PORTIONS
- PROVIDES CALCIUM, FOLATE, VITS B_1, C, D, & E

110g (4oz) strawberries, quartered

110g (4oz) raspberries

1 tbsp caster sugar

200ml (7fl oz) double or whipping cream

½ tsp pure vanilla extract

1 tsp icing sugar

4 tbsp Greek yogurt

2 ginger nut biscuits (optional)

Purée the berries with the caster sugar in a blender or food processor. Taste for sweetness and add a little more caster sugar if necessary. Sieve the purée to remove the seeds and set aside. Whip the cream with the vanilla extract and icing sugar until it holds soft peaks. Gently fold in the yogurt, then stir through the purée – it is nice to leave the purée slightly marbled in the cream mixture.

Spoon into small glasses, cover, and refrigerate until needed. (The fools can be kept in the fridge for up to 2 days.) If you like ginger, then these are nice with ginger nut biscuits crumbled over just before serving, though smaller babies may prefer it without the biscuits.

date baby first tried ....

baby's reaction ....

....

....

....

what I thought ....

....

....

my variations ....

....

....

....

....

....

tick
reaction

my favourite frozen yogurt

I adore frozen yogurt and this tastes so good that you don't really need any extra flavourings. However, if you like, you could add a fruit purée such as the summer berry flavour below. For best results, make this in an ice-cream machine, although you can also make it without. Simply put the mixture in a suitable container in the freezer, and then whiz in an electric mixer or food processor two or three times during the freezing process to break up the ice crystals.

- PREPARATION: 30 MINUTES (INCLUDING CHURNING), PLUS 3–4 HOURS FREEZING
- COOKING: NONE
- MAKES 750ML (1¼PINTS)
- PROVIDES CALCIUM, VITS A, D, & E

500g (1lb 2oz) full-fat natural yogurt
250ml (9fl oz) double cream
100g (3½oz) caster sugar

Simply mix all the ingredients together and freeze in an ice-cream machine. Transfer to a suitable container and keep in the freezer. If possible, remove from the freezer about 10 minutes before serving.

Variation: Summer berry frozen yogurt
Gently simmer 225g (8oz) fresh or frozen berries (e.g. strawberries, raspberries, blueberries, or blackberries) with about 2 tbsp icing sugar (to taste), then purée in a blender. Press through a sieve to remove the seeds. Mix the fruit purée with the yogurt mixture before freezing in an ice-cream machine. Alternatively, omit the cooking and simply purée fresh berries, then sieve and beat in about 2 tbsp icing sugar to sweeten. Makes 800ml (1⅓ pints).

" Try mixing other flavours into the yogurt base. Use a mango purée, mixed with a little sugar, or sieve some tinned lychees to make a delicious lychee frozen yogurt "

raspberry ripple ice lollies

Sucking on an ice lolly will help soothe sore gums when your child is teething. A lolly is also good if your child is feeling unwell and off his food, preventing her from becoming dehydrated. But then who needs an excuse to eat this yummy concoction of frozen yogurt rippled with fresh raspberry purée? I have whisked the yogurt mixture to improve the texture, but this is optional.

- PREPARATION: 15–20 MINUTES, PLUS OVERNIGHT FREEZING
- COOKING: NONE
- MAKES 600ML (1 PINT)
- PROVIDES CALCIUM, FOLATE, VITS C, D, & E

170g (6oz) raspberries
5 tbsp icing sugar
340g (12oz) vanilla yogurt
170ml (6fl oz) double cream

Purée the raspberries with 2 tbsp of the icing sugar in a blender or food processor. Sieve to remove the seeds and set aside.

Mix the yogurt, double cream, and remaining icing sugar in a large bowl. Whisk for 1–2 minutes with an electric mixer until thick and increased by about half in volume.

Stir 6 tbsp of the yogurt mixture into the raspberry purée. Spoon this raspberry mixture on to the yogurt mixture and roughly ripple through using the blade of a knife (don't overmix as it will mix a bit more as you pour it). Spoon or pour into ice lolly moulds and freeze.

strawberry-cranberry ice lollies

The strawberry is packed with vitamin C! If your strawberries are very ripe then you may need slightly less sugar.

- PREPARATION: 8–10 MINUTES, PLUS OVERNIGHT FREEZING
- COOKING: NONE
- MAKES ABOUT 600ML (1 PINT)
- PROVIDES BETA-CAROTENE, FOLATE, VITS B_1, B_2, B_3, & C

500g (1lb 2oz) strawberries, quartered
300ml (10fl oz) cranberry juice
55g (2oz) icing sugar, sifted

Whiz the strawberries, cranberry juice, and sugar together in a blender until smooth. Sieve to remove any seeds, then pour into lolly moulds and freeze.

date baby first tried ....

baby's reaction ....

what I thought ....

my variations ....

tick reaction

date baby first tried ....

baby's reaction ....

what I thought ....

my variations ....

tick reaction

date baby first tried ....

baby's reaction ....

....

....

....

what I thought ....

....

....

....

my variations ....

....

....

....

....

tick
reaction

iced banana smoothie sticks

This is a good way to use up the overripe bananas that always seem to be hiding in the bottom of the fruit bowl. For a special treat you can add a little *dulce de leche* (a South American milk-based syrup) to the mix, or dip the smoothie sticks in a little melted chocolate.

- PREPARATION: 5 MINUTES, PLUS OVERNIGHT FREEZING
- COOKING: NONE
- MAKES ABOUT 500ML (17FL OZ)
- PROVIDES CALCIUM, POTASSIUM, VITS A, C, D, & E

2 large, ripe bananas, peeled (250–280g/9–10oz peeled weight)

170g (6oz) vanilla yogurt

200ml (7fl oz) milk

Whiz the banana and yogurt together in a blender until smooth, then add the milk and whiz to combine. Pour into lolly moulds and freeze.

date baby first tried ....

baby's reaction ....

....

....

....

what I thought ....

....

....

my variations ....

....

....

....

....

tick
reaction

strawberry milkshake ice lollies

I like to make this using small probiotic strawberry yogurt drinks.

- PREPARATION: 8–10 MINUTES, PLUS OVERNIGHT FREEZING
- COOKING: NONE
- MAKES ABOUT 600ML (1 PINT)
- PROVIDES CALCIUM, VITS A, C, & D

250g (9oz) strawberries, quartered

350g (12oz) strawberry yogurt

100ml (3½fl oz) milk

3 tbsp icing sugar, sifted

Put the strawberries in a blender and whiz to a purée. Add the remaining ingredients and blend until frothy. Sieve to remove the strawberry seeds, then pour into lolly moulds and freeze.

" Babies who are teething very often go off their food. Sucking an enticing ice lolly can be good as it helps to soothe sore gums "

meal planner: energy boosters

This meal planner provides suggestions for your toddler's meals, many of which are drawn from this book. Either use the planner pages to map out your toddler's meals for the next weeks or to keep a record of your child's diet week-by-week.

breakfast	lunch	dinner	extras
porridge with honey fruit	First fish pie (pp120–121) fruit	Muffin pizza with hidden vegetable tomato sauce (pp152–152) First fruit fool (pp132–133)	Parmesan and herb pita crisps (p118); carrot and cucumber sticks and dip e.g. hummus
scrambled egg on wholegrain toast fruit	Pasta with simple squash and cheese sauce (p123) fruit	Chicken parmigiana (pp124–125) Bananas "foster" (p131)	Finger food sandwiches (pp90–92) yogurt
cereal fruit smoothie fromage frais	Hidden vegetable bolognaise with pasta (pp126–127); Strawberry-cranberry ice lollies (p135)	Goujons of fish (p115) with oven-baked chips and peas Orchard crumble (p130)	Parmesan and herb pita crisps (p118); carrot and cucumber sticks and dip e.g. hummus
French toast fingers (p89) mango or peach	Quick chicken risotto (p123) Orchard crumble (p130)	Muffin pizza with hidden vegetable tomato sauce (p152); Coconut rice pudding (p131)	Toasted peanut butter and banana sandwich (p119) yogurt
wheat-based cereal banana	Cheese and peas orzo (p122) First fruit fool (pp132–133)	Cute cottage pie (p169) fruit	Bomb (banana, oats, maple, and blueberry) muffin (pp116–117) fruit
toast fruit yogurt	Tuna tortilla melt (p119) My favourite frozen yogurt (p134) fruit	Hidden vegetable bolognaise with pasta (pp126–127); Raspberry ripple ice lollies (p135)	dried fruit e.g. apricots and raisins yogurt
Cheesy scrambled eggs (p97) fruit	Toasted peanut butter and banana sandwich (p119) fruit	My first sweet and sour pork (p164) Strawberry milkshake ice lolly (p136)	Ginger biscuit shapes (p129) yogurt fruit

● fishy favourites

Goujons of fish (p115) are a great way to tempt your little one into eating fish. They can be cooked from frozen too – perfect for when you're short of time.

WEEK 1	breakfast	lunch	dinner	extras
day 1				
day 2				
day 3				
day 4				
day 5				
day 6				
day 7				

meal planner: weeks 2 and 3

Use these planners to record the meals you give your toddler over the following weeks. If you want to record your child's meals for longer than three weeks, simply photocopy this page. Pieces of fruit or yogurt are good for snacks or desserts.

WEEK 2	breakfast	lunch	dinner	extras
day 1				
day 2				
day 3				
day 4				
day 5				
day 6				
day 7				

● individual portions

Your child will love individual child-sized portions of foods, such as My first fruit fool, right (see pages 132–133) and First fish pie (see pages 120–121).

WEEK 3	breakfast	lunch	dinner	extras
day 1				
day 2				
day 3				
day 4				
day 5				
day 6				
day 7				

other favourites

Use this page to note down your other favourite recipes, ideas for healthy and energy-boosting snacks, or recipe recommendations from your friends and family. It will be much easier to include your child in family meals, so enjoy experimenting!

foods my child loves and hates

Children have preferences from a young age. If your child rejects a food, try it again in a few weeks, in a totally different recipe.

Use this page to record your child's likes and dislikes. You'll find it will be amusing to look back on in years to come.

fussy eaters: 18–36 months

"Almost all children go through a stage of fussy eating. This can be very stressful, so here are my top tips on how to cope and some favourite recipes to tempt your child, which the whole family can enjoy."

healthy habits

Children of this age have a strong sense of self and can be fiercely independent. They often insist on having their own way, so you may find that your child, who used to eat so well, suddenly becomes very picky.

Don't despair, though, as your child gets a little older you may find he becomes more appreciative of food and can be completely absorbed by the food he eats. You'll be surprised how quiet a group of children can be around a table of yummy goodies or a birthday party spread.

● coping with a fussy eater

Whether they reject random recipes with butternut squash, visible onions, "hidden" courgette, "naked" chicken without breadcrumbs,

or chocolate brownies with nuts, let's face it, fuss is high on the menu for most children. Refusing foods is a normal part of growing up and is one of the first ways children can flex their muscles and assert their independence.

One thing is for sure, if your child refuses to eat, he will soon find that there is not much point making a fuss if you don't react. The problem is that this is stressful for you and you need to pretend that you actually don't care at all. Remove uneaten food without comment and offer nothing, despite the screams, tears, and tantrums. This will be difficult to handle, but it's not cruel. When it works you should have a happier, healthier child (and be less frazzled yourself). You will need help and support with this, so the whole family has to be in agreement and stick to the plan (even grandma!). Praise your child when he eats well or tries something new. You may need to ignore some bad eating behaviour to refocus attention on good behaviour.

● faddy eating

Many children go through phases of refusing to eat certain foods or refusing to eat anything at all. If your child only wants to eat a few favourite foods, try to build on a favourite food and work in others. If your child likes pasta, for example, make noodles with vegetables and chicken or spaghetti with meatballs.

It is very rare for a healthy child to starve himself. Even if your child goes through a few days of virtually eating nothing, he should start eating again very soon. He won't harm himself if he doesn't eat for a short while. The best thing to do is to offer a wide range of healthy, tasty meals – don't let your child pick. Also, cut out all unhealthy foods and minimize snacks.

● making vegetables tempting

Vegetables come pretty much top of the hate list and it may seem impossible to get your child to eat his five-a-day, when he won't even eat one or two. Here are some suggestions:

✱ **Finger foods** are popular with kids. Corn on the cob and sweet potato wedges are good choices.

✱ **If your child likes cheese**, make dishes like cauliflower and broccoli cheese or macaroni cheese with broccoli.

✱ **Instead of boring mashed potato**, mash some potato and carrot together with a little butter, milk, and seasoning.

✱ **Children often like stir-fries**, and you can pack these full of vegetables, such as finely sliced carrot and mangetout. Just stir in some noodles and teriyaki sauce.

✱ **Crunchy raw vegetables** are often more appealing than cooked vegetables. Try your child with carrot and cucumber sticks and slices of sweet pepper with a tasty dip. If you are out and about, wrap them in kitchen paper to keep them from drying out.

✱ **If all else fails, disguise vegetables**. Blend them into a tomato sauce for pasta (see the Hidden vegetable bolognaise recipe on pages 126–127). You could also try chopping vegetables

foods for fussy kids

My little girl of 18 months used to eat so well, but has recently become a fussy eater. Do you have any suggestions for what I can feed her?

Without going to unnecessary lengths, try to make your child's food not only taste good, but look good too. Make mini portions in ramekins, such as the Mini chicken pies (pages 160–161) and First fish pie (pages 120–121),

make chicken skewers or thread bite-sized pieces of fruit on to a straw. You could also try making your own healthy versions of popular foods, for example Muffin pizzas with hidden vegetable tomato sauce (pages 152–153) or fresh fruit ice lollies (pages 174–175). I also find that kids really enjoy ethnic-style foods. Try making Nasi goreng (page 157) or Chicken enchiladas (pages 158–159).

ask annabel

tips

If your child is a fussy eater, encourage good behaviour by praising him when he eats well or tries something new

Cooking with your children is a great way to get them to try new foods. Set a good example by making tasty, healthy foods

Do not give your child low-fat foods, such as skimmed milk or low-fat yogurt, before the age of two

into small pieces and hiding them inside a wrap. Just cover with tomato sauce and grated cheese and brown under the grill.

✳ **Remember that frozen vegetables** are as good as fresh. Try giving your child a mixture of frozen peas and sweetcorn.

✳ **Don't give up on salad.** Make one with cucumber, cherry tomato, shredded iceberg lettuce, grated carrot, and sweetcorn, and serve with a tasty dressing. Whisk together one tablespoon of balsamic vinegar, one tablespoon of soy sauce, a pinch each of caster sugar and dried mustard, four tablespoons of light olive oil, and some freshly ground black pepper.

✳ **Make a star chart.** Every time your child eats a new vegetable, put a star on the chart. When a whole line is filled with stars, reward him with a treat such as a trip to a theme park or a little toy.

● overweight children

At around the age of two or three children can become overweight. Young children need plenty of nourishment, so unless your child is seriously overweight, don't take drastic measures. Your aim should be to keep your child's weight steady and as he grows, he will slim down. If you think your child is seriously overweight, however, you should

seek professional help. Obesity is becoming a huge problem across the world (see below). We need to reverse this trend and encourage our

global obesity crisis

✳ **Over the past three decades**, the obesity rate in the United States has almost doubled for preschool children. In the UK, the obesity rate for two to three year olds has risen by almost a third in eight years.

✳ **A recent report**, written by 250 leading scientists, says that Britain's obesity crisis is so severe that if current trends continue, by 2050 about 60 per cent of men, 50 per cent of women, and 25 per cent of children in the UK will be clinically obese.

✳ **The report expects type 2 diabetes** to rise by 70 per cent, strokes by 30 per cent, and incidences of coronary heart disease by 20 per cent in the UK.

✳ **Obesity affects many countries** of the world. Scientists predict that the number of overweight children will increase significantly over the next few years in Southeast Asia, the Middle East, and South America, for example.

children to eat healthily and make good food choices from a young age. It can be difficult, especially when your child pesters you for unhealthy food; follow my strategies for encouraging healthy eating, below.

encouraging healthy eating

✳ **Start the day well**. It's not good for your child to go to nursery on an empty stomach. Your child needs energy and concentration until lunch. Wholegrain cereals, such as porridge, release sugars slowly, avoiding the highs and lows of sugary refined cereals. Read labels carefully and check that the cereal contains less than 10g (1/3 oz) of sugar per 100g (3½oz).

✳ **Set a good example**. You can't expect your child to eat well if you graze in front of the television and live off junk food and takeaways. It can take just 15 minutes to make a delicious meal for the whole family. Cook food from scratch so your child gets used to seeing you using a range of healthy ingredients. Eat meals together when possible, and don't let your child get into the habit of snacking in front of the television.

✳ **Don't pander to fussy eaters**. The more you give in to your child, offering only a few favourites like chicken nuggets, chips, and pizza, the more fussy your child will become.

✳ **Watch what you drink**. You can switch from full-fat to semi-skimmed milk once your child is two. It contains the same amount of calcium as full-fat milk. Make sure your child drinks enough water and limit juices.

● cook with your children

Most children love to cook and a good way to get them to try new foods and to enjoy healthy meals is to encourage them to have a hand in preparing food. Children love to help with cracking eggs, kneading and rolling out dough, or mixing batters.

Cooking is a great way of bonding with your child, and it's educational too. He will learn lots of new skills such as counting, weighing, measuring, and telling the time.

Involve your child in making the recipes in this section. He can help spread the tomato sauce on to the muffins and make shapes with the cheese for the Muffin pizzas (pages 152–153), for example.

● the importance of exercise

All children need daily exercise and, although most toddlers and small children are on the go all day, some may need a little more persuasion to be active. Even if they need little encouragement, it's worth getting your children into the habit of staying active as early as possible to make exercise part of their daily lives as they get older.

Get fit together – take your little one to the park and let him run around or take him on a short walk to the shops or to playgroup. If you feel your child is quite sedentary in his activities, try to replace quieter pastimes such as watching television or playing with toy bricks or dolls with more energetic ones, for example playing tag in the garden or dancing to music.

If your child is at nursery or with a childminder while you're at work, find out how much exercise he is getting during the day. Make sure he has regular activity periods and space to run and play.

strategies that worked for me

Use this space to record the ways you encourage your little one to eat healthily – whether it's recipe ideas for sneaking vegetables into your child's diet, healthy snacks that your child enjoys, or strategies for dealing with your little fussy eater.

date first tried.......................................

reaction ....
....
....
....
....

what I thought ....
....
....
....

my variations ....
....
....
....
....
....
....

tick
reaction

muffin pizza with hidden vegetable tomato sauce

My children love these mini pizzas. They even eat them for breakfast sometimes! I have puréed the veg and tomatoes before cooking, because it is easier to blend when there is more liquid and then it will be easier to tell when the sauce is thick enough.

- PREPARATION: 10 MINUTES
- COOKING: 30–35 MINUTES
- MAKES 1 PORTION
- PROVIDES PROTEIN, CALCIUM, BETA-CAROTENE, VITS C & D, PREBIOTICS
- SAUCE SUITABLE FOR FREEZING

1 large shallot, finely chopped

½ small leek, thinly sliced

1 small carrot, peeled and grated

¼ courgette, grated

1 tbsp olive oil

1 small clove garlic, crushed

2 tbsp tomato purée

1 tbsp sundried tomato purée

2 tbsp tomato ketchup

1 x 400g (14oz) tin chopped tomatoes

1½ tsp caster sugar

Salt and pepper

1 English muffin, split in half

30g (1oz) Cheddar or mozzarella cheese, grated

Put the vegetables in a large saucepan with the oil and sauté them for 8–10 minutes until soft but not coloured. Add the garlic and cook for 1 minute. Transfer to a blender. Add the purées, ketchup, tomatoes, and sugar, and whiz until smooth. Return to the pan and simmer, stirring occasionally, for about 20 minutes until thick. Season with salt and pepper, then allow to cool slightly.

Preheat the grill to high. Toast the base of the muffin halves. Turn them over, then spread 1 tbsp of sauce on each cut surface. Scatter over the cheese (or arrange in a pattern). Grill for 2–3 minutes until the cheese is melted and bubbling. Cool slightly, then cut into fingers or squares to serve. For older children you can leave the muffin halves whole or cut them in half.

Note: There will be lots of leftover sauce, but it freezes very well, for up to 3 months. Freeze in individual portions so that you can thaw it quickly. This also makes a delicious sauce for pasta and it's a good way to get children to eat more vegetables, because what they can't see, they can't pick out. For a pasta sauce, cut down the cooking time so the sauce is not so thick.

date first tried.............................

reaction..

what I thought.............................

my variations...............................

tick
reaction

chicken balls with spaghetti and tomato sauce

Chicken balls flavoured with apple are a signature dish of mine. Lots of mums tell me how popular they are with their children. Delicious with spaghetti and tomato sauce, they can also be served as finger food. If you are freezing this, freeze the chicken balls and tomato sauce separately in individual portions and then cook the spaghetti fresh.

- PREPARATION: 25 MINUTES
- COOKING: 20 MINUTES
- MAKES 5–6 PORTIONS
- PROVIDES PROTEIN, IRON, SELENIUM, ZINC, CALCIUM, BETA-CAROTENE, FOLATE, VIT D, PREBIOTICS
- SUITABLE FOR FREEZING

Tomato sauce

1–2 tbsp olive oil

2 onions, finely chopped

1 clove garlic, crushed

1 x 400g (14oz) tin chopped tomatoes

1 tbsp tomato purée

2 tsp sugar

¼ tsp dried oregano

Chicken balls

250g (9oz) minced chicken

1 small apple, peeled and grated

1 tsp fresh thyme leaves

25g (scant 1oz) Parmesan cheese, freshly grated

30g (1oz) fresh white breadcrumbs

Salt and pepper

Plain flour to dust hands

3 tbsp sunflower oil, for frying

To serve

25g (scant 1oz) spaghetti per portion

Chopped fresh parsley or basil

Heat the oil in a saucepan and gently fry the onions for about 10 minutes until softened. Spoon half the onions into a bowl and leave to cool (these will be used for the chicken balls). Add the garlic to the onions left in the pan and sauté for 1 minute, then add all the remaining sauce ingredients plus 100ml (3½fl oz) water. Cover and simmer for 7–8 minutes, stirring occasionally.

Meanwhile, to make the chicken balls, add the mince, grated apple, thyme, and Parmesan to the onions in the bowl. Add the breadcrumbs and season with salt and pepper. Mix together well. With floured hands, form teaspoons of the mixture into about 20–24 small balls. Heat the sunflower oil in a frying pan and brown the balls all over. Transfer the balls to the pan of tomato sauce and simmer uncovered for 8–10 minutes.

Cook the spaghetti according to the instructions on the packet. Drain and toss with the chicken balls and sauce. Sprinkle with a little parsley or basil.

> "Try making these with minced turkey or beef as a tasty alternative to chicken"

date first tried ....

reaction ....

....

....

....

....

what I thought ....

....

....

my variations ....

....

....

....

....

....

....

tick
reaction

pasta salad with pesto dressing

I have made two different dressings to go with this salad. The first one is creamier as it uses mayonnaise. If you are taking this salad out on a picnic, then you might prefer to use the second dressing made with olive oil, and some of the less perishable add-ins.

- PREPARATION: 10 MINUTES
- COOKING: 12 MINUTES
- MAKES 2 PORTIONS
- PROVIDES PROTEIN, CALCIUM, IRON, BETA-CAROTENE, FOLATE, VITS A, B_1, B_3, C, & D, PREBIOTICS

55g (2oz) pasta spirals

Dressing 1

1½ tbsp mayonnaise

1½ tbsp pesto

3–4 drops of lemon juice

Dressing 2

1 tbsp olive oil

2 tsp pesto

3–4 drops of lemon juice

Add-ins

55g (2oz) cooked chicken, shredded (see page 96)

55g (2oz) Cheddar cheese, cubed

55g (2oz) cooked ham, cut into thin strips

1 medium tomato, deseeded and cut into strips

1 spring onion, thinly sliced

¼ red or orange pepper, cut into strips

Small handful of cooked broccoli florets

2cm (¾in) piece of cucumber, cut into matchsticks

Cook the pasta according to the packet instructions. Meanwhile, mix together the ingredients for dressing 1 or 2. Drain the pasta and rinse well with cold water, then toss in the dressing. Mix in two or three add-ins of your choice. Keep the salad in the fridge until needed.

nasi goreng

A delicious Indonesian recipe.

- PREPARATION: 15 MINUTES
- COOKING: 15 MINUTES
- MAKES 4 PORTIONS
- PROVIDES PROTEIN, IRON, MAGNESIUM, ZINC, VITS A, D, & E, PREBIOTICS

1 skinless, boneless chicken breast, diced

125g (4½oz) long-grain rice

1½ tbsp vegetable oil

1 tsp toasted sesame oil

2 shallots or 1 onion, finely chopped

1 small clove garlic, crushed

½ small red pepper, finely chopped

½ tbsp chopped fresh parsley

½ tbsp mild curry powder

¼ tsp turmeric

Small pinch of mild chilli powder

4 tbsp chicken stock

50g (scant 2oz) frozen peas

2 small spring onions, finely sliced

½ tbsp soft dark brown sugar

25g (scant 1oz) roasted peanuts, finely chopped

Marinade

1½ tbsp soy sauce

1 tsp toasted sesame oil

½ tbsp soft dark brown sugar

Omelette

1 egg

¼ tsp caster sugar

Small pinch of salt

1 tsp sunflower oil

Marinate the chicken in the soy sauce, sesame oil, and sugar for 30 minutes, then drain, reserving the marinade. While the chicken is marinating, cook the rice according to the packet instructions.

To make the omelette, beat together the egg, sugar, salt, and ½ tsp cold water. Heat the oil in a small non-stick frying pan. Pour in the egg mixture and swirl to cover the bottom of the pan in a thin layer. Cook for about 1 minute until set, then turn over and cook for 30 seconds on the other side. Remove the omelette from the pan and cut into strips. Set aside.

Heat the oils in a wok or frying pan and sauté the shallots for 3 minutes. Add the garlic and cook for 30 seconds. Add the red pepper and sauté for 2 minutes, then add the parsley and chicken. Cook for 3 minutes. Stir in the curry powder, turmeric, and chilli powder with the reserved marinade and the stock. Cook for 1 minute. Add the peas and spring onions and cook for 2 minutes. Stir in the rice, sugar, peanuts, and omelette, and heat through.

Note: Keep leftovers in the fridge for up to 24 hours. Add ½ tsp water and microwave for 1–2 minutes until piping hot. Cool slightly before serving.

date first tried ....

reaction ....

what I thought ....

my variations ....

tick reaction

date first tried ....

reaction ....

....

....

....

what I thought ....

....

....

my variations ....

....

....

....

....

....

tick
reaction

annabel's chicken enchiladas

Wraps are the new trendy food and are very popular with children. An enchilada is a Mexican wrap – a flour tortilla rolled around a filling, covered with a sauce and grated cheese, and baked. It's a great way to sneak some extra veggies into the diet. All my children love it.

- PREPARATION: 25–30 MINUTES
- COOKING: 45 MINUTES
- MAKES 8 ENCHILADAS
- PROVIDES PROTEIN, IRON, SELENIUM, ZINC, CALCIUM, FOLATE, VITS A, C, & D, PREBIOTICS
- SUITABLE FOR FREEZING

8 small flour tortilla wraps

Tomato sauce

1 tbsp olive oil

1 red onion, finely chopped

1 clove garlic, crushed

½ tsp dried oregano

1 x 400g (14oz) tin chopped tomatoes

1 tbsp tomato purée

1 tbsp sundried tomato purée

1 tsp caster sugar

Chicken filling

1 tbsp olive oil

1 clove garlic, crushed

1 red onion, chopped

1 red pepper, deseeded and diced

1 small courgette, diced

350g (12oz) minced chicken

200g (7oz) Cheddar cheese, grated

To make the sauce, heat the oil in a large saucepan and sauté the onion for 5 minutes until soft. Add the garlic and cook for 1 minute, then add the remaining sauce ingredients. Bring to the boil and simmer for 20 minutes until thick, stirring occasionally. Season and blend until smooth.

Make the chicken filling while the sauce is simmering. Heat the olive oil in a large frying pan or wok and stir in the garlic, onion, red pepper, and courgette. Cook for 5 minutes, then add the chicken and season with salt and pepper. Continue to cook, stirring occasionally, for 7–8 minutes until the chicken is cooked through. Stir in half of the cheese until melted.

Preheat the oven to 200°C (180°C fan), gas 6. Lightly oil a large ovenproof dish.

Warm the tortillas slightly (in the oven or microwave), then divide the filling among them, spooning it down the centre. Roll up the tortillas and arrange, seam side down and in one layer, in the dish. Spoon over the sauce and sprinkle on the remaining cheese. Bake for 15–20 minutes until bubbling and the cheese is golden brown. Cool to warm before serving.

Note: Freeze (in individual portions) unbaked, without the cheese; thaw overnight in the fridge, then add the cheese before baking.

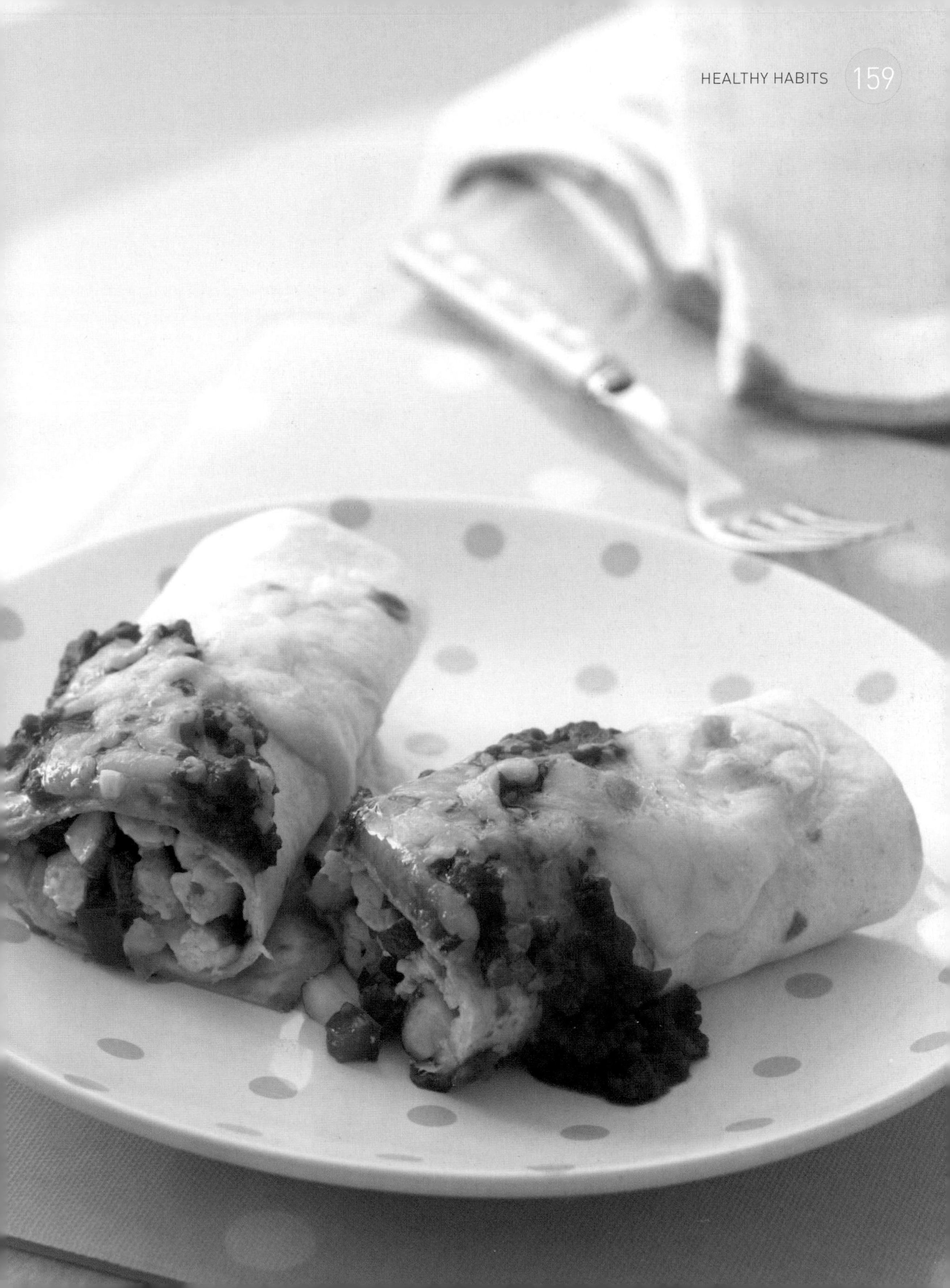

mini chicken pies

Sweating the vegetables slowly with thyme and then reducing the white wine vinegar gives a lovely flavour to the filling for these pies. If you cut the chicken across the grain into thin slices, it breaks up the fibres and helps make the chicken very tender. The pies freeze well so you can bake and serve one, and freeze the other three. Or bake in larger dishes to feed the whole family.

- PREPARATION: 25–30 MINUTES
- COOKING: 30–35 MINUTES
- MAKES 4 INDIVIDUAL PIES
- PROVIDES PROTEIN, IRON, POTASSIUM, ZINC, BETA-CAROTENE, VITS D & E
- SUITABLE FOR FREEZING

45g (1½oz) butter

1 small shallot, diced

1 medium carrot, peeled and diced

½ small leek, thinly sliced

¼ tsp chopped fresh thyme leaves

4 tsp white wine vinegar

20g (¾oz) cornflour

400ml (14fl oz) hot chicken stock

2 tbsp crème fraîche

Salt and pepper

500g (1lb 2oz) potatoes, peeled and cubed

3 tbsp milk

225g (8oz) skinless, boneless chicken breast, cut into thin, bite-size slices

1 egg white, lightly beaten (optional)

Melt 30g (1oz) butter and sweat the vegetables with the thyme for 10 minutes until soft. Add the vinegar and boil until it has evaporated. Stir in the cornflour, then add the stock a little at a time, stirring, to make a smooth sauce. Add the crème fraîche and season to taste with salt and pepper. Allow the sauce to cool.

Cook the potatoes in plenty of boiling salted water for about 15 minutes until just tender. Drain the potatoes, then mash well. Beat in the remaining butter and the milk, and season to taste.

Divide the chicken among four ramekins or small ovenproof dishes (I use 9.5cm/scant 4in diameter ramekins) and spoon the sauce on top. Cover with the mash and fork the surface to mark lines.

Preheat the oven to 200°C (180°C fan), gas 6. Put the dish(es) on a baking tray and bake for 30 minutes. If the pies are fridge-cold, bake for an extra 5 minutes. The tops can be browned further under a hot grill – if you brush them with a little egg white, they will brown nicely.

Note: To freeze, wrap the potato-topped pies well; thaw overnight in the fridge before baking.

teriyaki salmon

Eating food on a stick is always more fun than using a fork or spoon (although for small children it is safer to remove the salmon from the skewers to serve), and this is a tasty way to get your child to eat more oily fish. The cooked skewers can be kept in the fridge for up to two days, and are nice cold, so good for lunchboxes.

- PREPARATION: 10 MINUTES, PLUS 30 MINUTES TO SOAK SKEWERS
- COOKING: 6 MINUTES
- MAKES 6 PORTIONS
- PROVIDES PROTEIN, OMEGA-3s, IRON, SELENIUM, VITS D & E

1 tbsp sesame seeds

200g (7oz) piece of skinless, boneless salmon fillet

¼ tsp grated fresh root ginger

1 tbsp clear honey

1½ tsp soy sauce

Put six wooden skewers to soak in cold water for 30 minutes. Meanwhile, toast the sesame seeds in a small frying pan over a medium heat for 2–3 minutes, stirring two or three times. Spread out on a plate and cool.

Preheat the grill to high. Cut the salmon into 1cm (½in) cubes. Thread three or four cubes on to each skewer and lay the skewers in one layer on a foil-lined baking tray.

Mix the ginger with the honey and soy sauce. Brush some of this teriyaki sauce on to the salmon and grill for 2 minutes, as close to the heat as possible. Brush again with the teriyaki sauce and grill for another 2 minutes. Turn the skewers over and repeat the brushing and grilling process.

Sprinkle the sesame seeds over the salmon before serving.

Variation: Add 1 tsp sweet chilli sauce to the teriyaki sauce.

date first tried.............

reaction.............

what I thought.............

my variations.............

tick reaction

"Try to include oily fish in your child's diet twice a week. Other good ways to serve it are in fish pies or fishcakes"

my first sweet and sour pork

Small children will find minced pork a little easier to eat than cubes, and they often don't notice the vegetables in this! Serve with rice.

- PREPARATION: 10 MINUTES
- COOKING: 8 MINUTES
- MAKES 2 PORTIONS
- PROVIDES PROTEIN, IRON, SELENIUM, MANGANESE, ZINC, FOLATE, VITS A, B_3, & C, PREBIOTICS
- SUITABLE FOR FREEZING

2 tbsp tomato ketchup

1½ tsp soy sauce

2 tbsp pineapple juice (from the tin)

1 tsp cornflour

1 tbsp sunflower oil

110g (4oz) minced pork (or chicken)

2 spring onions, thinly sliced

¼ red pepper, diced

1 ring tinned pineapple, diced

2 tbsp tinned sweetcorn, drained

Mix together the ketchup, soy sauce, pineapple juice, cornflour, and 4 tbsp water in a small bowl. Set this sauce mixture aside.

Heat the sunflower oil in a wok and stir-fry the pork mince for 3 minutes, breaking it up well as you cook. Add the spring onions and red pepper, and cook for another 3 minutes until the vegetables are soft and the pork is browned. Add the pineapple, sweetcorn, and sauce mixture and cook for a further 1–2 minutes until the sauce is bubbling and thickened.

egg fried rice with chicken and prawns

Children like egg fried rice. You can make it with other vegetables like diced steamed carrot, or leave out the prawns and add extra chicken.

- PREPARATION: 15 MINUTES, PLUS 30 MINUTES MARINATING
- COOKING: 8 MINUTES
- MAKES 4 PORTIONS
- PROVIDES PROTEIN, IRON, SELENIUM, ZINC, FOLATE, VITS A, D, & E, PREBIOTICS

150g (5½oz) skinless, boneless chicken, cut into small cubes

175g (6oz) basmati rice

2 tbsp sunflower oil

1 small onion, finely chopped

60g (generous 2oz) frozen peas

1 large spring onion, finely sliced

125g (4½oz) cooked prawns

Marinade

1 tbsp soy sauce

½ tsp caster sugar

1 tsp cornflour

Omelette

1 tsp sunflower oil

1 large egg, beaten with a pinch of salt

Mix together the marinade ingredients and marinate the chicken for at least 30 minutes. Meanwhile, cook the rice according to the packet instructions.

To make the omelette, heat the oil in a small frying pan. Add the beaten egg and tilt the pan so that the egg covers the bottom thinly. Cook until set. Transfer to a chopping board, roll up, and cut into strips. Set aside.

Heat the 2 tbsp oil in a wok and sauté the onion for 2 minutes. Add the chicken with its marinade and sauté for 2 more minutes. Add the frozen peas, spring onion, and prawns, and cook for 1 minute. Fluff up the rice with a fork, add to the wok with the omelette strips, and stir-fry for 1 minute.

Note: Leftovers can be kept in the fridge for up to 24 hours. Add ½ tsp water and microwave for 1–2 minutes until piping hot. Cool slightly before serving.

date first tried ....

reaction ....

....

....

what I thought ....

....

....

my variations ....

....

....

....

....

....

tick
reaction

thai-style chicken with noodles

I find that most children love noodles and you will be able to sneak in some veggies with them. Feel free to make up your own version using vegetables of your choice – mini broccoli florets would be good. It's fun to serve this in a bowl and let your child eat this using child-friendly chopsticks, which are joined at the top.

- PREPARATION: 15–20 MINUTES, PLUS 1 HOUR MARINATING
- COOKING: 8–10 MINUTES
- MAKES 4–6 PORTIONS
- PROVIDES PROTEIN, IRON, SELENIUM, ZINC, BETA-CAROTENE, FOLATE, VITS B_2 & C, PREBIOTICS
- SUITABLE FOR FREEZING

1 tsp fish sauce

½ tsp soy sauce

½ tsp caster sugar

225g (8oz) skinless, boneless chicken breasts, cut into small strips

100g (3½oz) fine egg noodles

3 tsp sunflower oil

1 small clove garlic, crushed

½ tsp grated fresh root ginger

25g (scant 1oz) shallot, thinly sliced

1½ tsp mild korma curry paste

1 small carrot, peeled and cut into fine matchsticks

Small handful of mange tout, cut into fine matchsticks

¼ red pepper, cut into fine matchsticks

100ml (3½fl oz) chicken stock

200ml (7fl oz) coconut milk

1 tsp lime juice

Salt and pepper (optional)

Mix together the fish sauce, soy sauce, and sugar in a medium bowl, stirring until the sugar has dissolved. Add the chicken and toss to coat. Leave to marinate for 1 hour. Meanwhile, cook the noodles according to the packet instructions, rinse with cold water, and drain well. Toss with 1 tsp of the oil.

Heat the remaining oil in a wok. Add the garlic, ginger, and shallot, and stir-fry for 1 minute. Add the chicken with its marinade and stir-fry for 3–4 minutes until the chicken is almost cooked. Mix in the curry paste followed by the vegetables, chicken stock, and coconut milk. Bring to the boil, then reduce the heat and simmer for 5 minutes until the vegetables are tender and the chicken is thoroughly cooked.

Add the noodles and toss in the sauce for 1–2 minutes, to reheat. Add the lime juice and season, if liked, with a little salt and pepper.

Note: Leftovers can be kept in the fridge for up to 2 days; reheat in the microwave (adding 1 tsp water per portion) for 1–2 minutes until piping hot. If frozen, thaw in the fridge overnight before reheating.

meatloaf with tangy bbq sauce

This is a moist and tender meatloaf. I have mixed the ingredients in a food processor to give a finer texture, which small children tend to prefer; however, you could just mix everything together in a bowl. With a "free-form" meatloaf, the yummy sauce can be brushed all over.

- PREPARATION: 15 MINUTES
- COOKING: 45 MINUTES
- MAKES 6 PORTIONS
- PROVIDES PROTEIN, IRON, SELENIUM, ZINC, VIT C, PREBIOTICS
- SUITABLE FOR FREEZING

Sauce

100ml (3½fl oz) tomato ketchup

2 tbsp maple syrup or clear honey

1 tsp soy sauce

1 tsp Worcestershire sauce

1 tsp balsamic vinegar

2 tbsp orange juice

Meatloaf

40g (scant 1½oz) fresh white breadcrumbs

6 tbsp milk

1 small red onion, finely diced

2 tsp olive oil

1 clove garlic, crushed

225g (8oz) minced beef or a mixture of beef and pork

¼ tsp dried oregano

Salt and pepper

Preheat the oven to 180°C (160°C fan), gas 4.

Mix the ketchup, maple syrup (or honey), soy sauce, Worcestershire sauce, and balsamic vinegar together in a medium saucepan. Transfer 3 tbsp of this mixture to a bowl, then add the orange juice to the saucepan. Set aside.

Mix the breadcrumbs and milk in a bowl and soak for 10 minutes. Meanwhile, sauté the onion in the oil for 5 minutes until translucent. Add the garlic and cook for a further minute. Transfer to a food processor and add the breadcrumbs, beef, oregano, and 2 tbsp of the sauce in the bowl. Season with salt and pepper, then whiz until well combined.

Spoon the mixture on to a baking tray lined with baking parchment and pat into a loaf shape roughly 20cm (8in) long and 8cm (just over 3in) wide. Bake for 20 minutes. Brush with half of the sauce left in the bowl and with any juices. Bake for another 20 minutes, then brush over the remaining sauce from the bowl and bake for a final 5 minutes.

Rest for 10 minutes before slicing (cut into bite-size cubes for toddlers). Heat the sauce in the pan until bubbling, to serve with the meatloaf.

Note: Freeze individual slices with sauce on top; thaw overnight in the fridge, then reheat in the microwave for 45–60 seconds.

cute cottage pies

Most children like grated carrot, but if your baby is particularly fussy about vegetables then sauté the carrot with the other vegetables and blend into the sauce. For younger babies it might be a good idea to transfer the cooked minced beef to a food processor and whiz for a few seconds to get a finer texture before adding it to the cooked vegetables.

- PREPARATION: 20 MINUTES
- COOKING: 20–25 MINUTES
- MAKES 4–6 INDIVIDUAL PIES
- PROVIDES PROTEIN, IRON, SELENIUM, ZINC, POTASSIUM, CALCIUM, BETA-CAROTENE, VITS C & D
- SUITABLE FOR FREEZING

3 tbsp olive oil

225g (8oz) lean minced beef

½ medium onion, chopped

½ medium leek, sliced

60g (generous 2oz) chestnut mushrooms, diced

2 sprigs of fresh thyme, leaves only

250ml (9fl oz) beef stock

2 tsp sundried tomato purée

1 tbsp soy sauce

1 tsp Worcestershire sauce

1 medium carrot, peeled and coarsely grated

500g (1lb 2oz) potatoes, peeled and cubed

15g (½oz) butter

3 tbsp milk

Salt and pepper

45g (1½oz) Cheddar cheese, grated

Heat 1 tbsp olive oil in a large non-stick frying pan and stir-fry the beef for 5–7 minutes until well browned and crumbly. Transfer to a bowl and set aside.

Add the remaining olive oil to the pan and sauté the onion, leek, and mushrooms with the thyme for 7–8 minutes until soft. Add the beef stock, then transfer to a blender and blend until smooth. Return to the frying pan along with the beef, and stir in the tomato purée, soy sauce, Worcestershire sauce, and carrot. Bring to the boil, then lower the heat and simmer for 10 minutes. Divide among four to six small ovenproof dishes or ramekins.

While the mince is simmering, cook the potatoes in boiling salted water for about 15 minutes until just tender. Drain, then mash well. Beat in the butter and milk and season to taste. Spoon the potato over the mince and fork the surface to make decorative lines. Sprinkle over the cheese.

Preheat the oven to 200°C (180°C fan), gas 6. Set the dish(es) on a baking tray and bake for 20 minutes until hot in the centre and golden on top. If the pies are fridge-cold, bake for an extra 5 minutes. The tops can be browned further under a hot grill, if you like.

Note: If freezing the pies, thaw overnight in the fridge before baking.

date first tried

reaction

what I thought

my variations

tick reaction

moroccan lamb

Here's a great recipe for batch cooking. Serve with couscous or rice.

- PREPARATION: 25 MINUTES
- COOKING: 1¾ HOURS
- MAKES 8–10 PORTIONS
- PROVIDES PROTEIN, IRON, SELENIUM, ZINC, VITS A, B_3, & C, PREBIOTICS
- SUITABLE FOR FREEZING

500g (1lb 2oz) leg of lamb, cubed

2 tbsp plain flour

Salt and pepper

2–3 tbsp sunflower oil

1 large onion, chopped

1 large clove garlic, crushed

1¼ tsp ground cinnamon

1½ tsp mild curry paste

600ml (1 pint) vegetable stock

1 x 400g (14oz) tin chopped tomatoes

5 tbsp tomato purée

1 tbsp mango chutney

½ eating apple, grated

150g (5½oz) ready-to-eat dried apricots, chopped

Toss the lamb cubes in seasoned flour. Heat the oil in a medium flameproof casserole and brown the lamb all over. Remove the lamb and set aside.

Add the onion to the pot and fry for 7–8 minutes until soft. Add the garlic, cinnamon, and curry paste and cook for 1 minute, then add any leftover flour and cook for 2 minutes. Remove from the heat and stir in the stock, a little at a time. Return the lamb to the casserole and stir in the tomatoes, tomato purée, mango chutney, and apple. Season to taste.

Set the pot over a medium heat and bring to a simmer. Cover and cook very gently for 1 hour, stirring occasionally. Add the apricots and continue to cook, uncovered, for a further 30–45 minutes until the lamb is tender.

mini croque monsieur

This is quite a generous portion for a child of 18 months but fine for two to three year olds. The trick is to roll out the bread slices thinly so that the sandwich is nice and crisp and not too thick for small mouths. You can also make variations such as using smoked turkey or chicken instead of ham, using all cheese (increase to 55g/2oz), or spreading a little tomato ketchup or yeast extract plus extra butter on the bread before adding the ham. Instead of grilling, you can cook the sandwich in a preheated non-stick frying pan over a medium heat.

- PREPARATION: 5 MINUTES
- COOKING: ABOUT 4 MINUTES
- MAKES 1 PORTION
- PROVIDES PROTEIN, IRON, SELENIUM, ZINC, CALCIUM

2 slices bread

1 slice cooked ham

Handful of grated Cheddar cheese (about 30g/1oz)

15g (½oz) butter, at room temperature

Preheat the grill to high.

Use a rolling pin to roll out the slices of bread so that they are nice and thin. Lay the ham on one slice of bread and scatter over the cheese. Top with the second slice of bread. Spread the butter in a thin layer over the outside on both sides of the sandwich, making sure you go right to the edges.

Grill the sandwich about 5cm (2in) from the heat source for about 2 minutes on each side until the bread is golden and the cheese has melted. Allow to cool slightly, then cut into fingers.

Variation: Try making ham and cheese quesadillas too. Sprinkle grated cheese on to a tortilla, cover with a layer of sliced ham, and sprinkle a little more cheese on top. Cover with another tortilla, and cook for 1½ minutes on each side in a dry frying pan. Cut into slices to serve.

date first tried ....
....
reaction ....
....
....
....
....
what I thought ....
....
....
....
my variations ....
....
....
....
....
....
....
....

tick reaction

" Kids will love these ham and cheese grilled sandwiches. Try them with chicken or turkey, or the delicious quesadilla variation too "

date first tried...

reaction...

....

....

what I thought ....

....

....

my variations ....

....

....

....

....

....

tick
reaction

apple and blackberry surprise

This is very tasty, a bit like a luxury porridge with caramelized apple and blackberry. You could halve the quantities to make enough for two children, but I'd stick to four – then you might get to eat some too!

- PREPARATION: 20 MINUTES
- COOKING: 20 MINUTES
- MAKES 4 PORTIONS
- PROVIDES CALCIUM, FOLATE, VITS A, B_1, B_2, B_3, C, & D, PREBIOTICS

50g (scant 2oz) butter

75g (2½oz) rolled oats

50g (scant 2oz) caster sugar

2 Granny Smith apples, peeled, cored, and sliced

150ml (5fl oz) whipping cream

115g (4oz) Greek yogurt

2 tbsp clear honey

2 tbsp light muscovado sugar

200g (7oz) blackberries

Melt half the butter in a small pan, add the oats, and cook for 1 minute. Stir in half the caster sugar and cook, stirring, for 4–5 minutes until the oats are lightly caramelized. Tip on to a baking tray, spread out, and leave to cool.

Melt the remaining butter in a large pan and sauté the apple slices for 3–4 minutes until they begin to soften. Add the remaining caster sugar and cook for a further 8–10 minutes until caramelized. Allow to cool.

Lightly whip the cream, then fold in the yogurt, honey, muscovado sugar, and oats. Reserve eight blackberries; stir the rest into the yogurt cream, crushing them slightly. Layer up the blackberry cream with the apples in four glasses and top with the reserved blackberries.

red fruit rocket lolly

It's so simple to make your own yummy fruit lollies. The amount of sugar you add will depend on how sweet the fruit is. If your berries and watermelon are very sweet, you can reduce the sugar by 1 tbsp.

- PREPARATION: 10 MINUTES, PLUS FREEZING
- COOKING: NONE
- MAKES 400ML (14FL OZ)
- PROVIDES POTASSIUM, BETA-CAROTENE, FOLATE, VITS B_6 & C

200g (7oz) strawberries, halved

200g (7oz) raspberries

150g (5½oz) cubed watermelon, deseeded

4 tbsp caster sugar

Blend everything together until smooth. Taste for sweetness and add a little extra sugar if needed. Sieve the mixture to remove the seeds, then pour into rocket-shaped ice lolly moulds and freeze.

mango and pineapple tropical lolly

Lollies are always a good way to get children to eat fruit. You need a very ripe mango for this.

- PREPARATION: 10 MINUTES, PLUS FREEZING
- COOKING: NONE
- MAKES 500ML (17FL OZ)
- PROVIDES MANGANESE, BETA-CAROTENE, FOLATE, VITS B_3 & C

1 x 225g (8oz) tin pineapple (rings or chunks), with juice

1 large ripe mango, peeled and pitted

4 tbsp icing sugar

1 tbsp coconut milk

1 tsp lime juice (or lemon)

Blend everything together until smooth. Pour into lolly moulds and freeze.

One way to get your child to eat more fruit is to make fresh fruit ice lollies. You can also freeze shop-bought fruit smoothies or juices

meal planner: healthy habits

This meal planner provides suggestions for your toddler's meals, many of which are drawn from this book. Either use the planner pages to map out your toddler's meals for the next weeks or to keep a record of your child's diet week-by-week.

breakfast	lunch	dinner	extras
wheat-based cereal yogurt fruit	Mini chicken pies (pp160–161) with broccoli Orchard crumble (p130)	Teriyaki salmon (pp162–163) with rice or vegetables fruit	rice cakes dried fruit yogurt
scrambled egg on wholegrain toast	My first sweet and sour pork (p164) Orchard crumble (p130)	Egg fried rice with chicken and prawns (p165) fruit	Mini croque monsieur (p171) fruit
porridge with honey fruit	Moroccan lamb (p170) with couscous My favourite frozen yogurt (p134); fruit	Muffin pizza (pp152–153) Apple and blackberry surprise (pp172–173)	carrot and cucumber sticks with a dip, e.g. hummus yogurt
fruit smoothie cereal fromage frais	Chicken balls with spaghetti and tomato sauce (pp154–155) fruit	stuffed baked potato with filling, e.g. cheese and ham; Mango and pineapple lolly (pp174–175)	cheese and grapes Ginger biscuit shapes (p129)
boiled egg with fingers of toast fruit	Goujons of fish (p115) with oven-baked chips Red fruit rocket lolly (pp174–175)	Annabel's chicken enchiladas (pp158–159) fruit	Finger food sandwiches (p90–92) Ginger biscuit shapes (p129); fruit
granola with yogurt, honey, and fruit	Pasta salad with pesto dressing (p156) fruit	Cute cottage pies (p169) My favourite frozen yogurt (p134) fruit	grilled cheese on toast yogurt fruit
pancakes or waffles with maple syrup berries	Thai-style chicken with noodles (pp166–167) fruit	Meatloaf with tangy BBQ sauce (p168) Bananas "Foster" (p131)	Mini oat and raisin biscuits (pp102–103) yogurt fruit

● hidden vegetables

Sometimes you need to be inventive to
encourage your child to eat vegetables. My first
sweet and sour pork (page 164) is full of such
lively flavours he may not spot the vegetables.

WEEK 1	breakfast	lunch	dinner	extras
day 1				
day 2				
day 3				
day 4				
day 5				
day 6				
day 7				

meal planner: weeks 2 and 3

Use these planners to record the meals you give your toddler over the following weeks. If you want to record your child's meals for longer than three weeks, simply photocopy this page. Pieces of fruit or yogurt make good snacks and desserts.

WEEK 2	breakfast	lunch	dinner	extras
day 1				
day 2				
day 3				
day 4				
day 5				
day 6				
day 7				

● eating with the family

Set a good example to your child by making delicious, healthy home-cooked meals that the whole family can enjoy. Take time to eat together as a family as often as you can.

WEEK 3	breakfast	lunch	dinner	extras
day 1				
day 2				
day 3				
day 4				
day 5				
day 6				
day 7				

other favourites

Use this page to note down your other favourite recipes, ideas for healthy and energy-boosting snacks, or recipe recommendations from your friends and family. It will be much easier to include your child in family meals, so enjoy experimenting!

foods my child loves and hates

Children have preferences from a young age. If your child rejects a food, try it again in a few weeks, in a totally different recipe.

Use this page to record your child's likes and dislikes. It will be amusing to look back on in years to come.

notes for growing up

Just because your little one has got to the age of three, doesn't mean you need to stop recording. Use this space to note down anything from your child's food likes and dislikes and food fads to favourite recipes and foods you cook together.

useful addresses

Allergy UK
3, White Oak Square
London Road
Swanley
Kent BR8 7AG
Tel: 01322619898
www.allergyuk.org
*A national medical charity
dealing with allergy, which
provides up-to-date information
on allergy, food intolerance, and
chemical sensitivity.*

Anaphylaxis Campaign
PO Box 275
Farnborough
Hampshire GU14 6SX
Tel: 01252 546100
Helpline: 01252 542029
www.anaphlaxis.org.uk
*A charity set up to help those in
the UK with life-threatening
allergic reactions to peanuts
and many other foods.*

akTV
http://annabelkarmel.tv
*A website packed full of video
clips of Annabel Karmel
demonstrating recipes, offering
advice on weaning and
superfoods, and answering
parents' Q&As.*

Annabel Karmel
49 Berkeley Square
London W1J 5AZ
Tel: 020 7355 4555
www.annabelkarmel.com
*Annabel's website includes
advice on weaning, recipes, and
a forum to discuss issues with
other parents and carers.
Purchase Annabel's other
books online too.*

**Association of Breastfeeding
Mothers**
PO Box 207
Bridgwater TA6 7YT
Tel: 08444 122949
www.abm.me.uk
counselling@abm.me.uk
*A charity run by mothers for
mothers, which gives helpful,
friendly advice and accurate
information to mothers who
breastfeed. Offers a telephone
and email counselling service
(see details above).*

BabyCentre
www.babycentre.co.uk
*An online community for new
parents, offering information
and advice on all aspects of
childcare up to 36 months.*

Boots
PO Box 5300
Nottingham NG90 1AA
Tel: 08450 708090
www.boots.com
*Stockists of useful kitchen
equipment and ingredients.*

Breastfeeding Network
PO Box 11126
Paisley
PA2 8YB
Tel: 0844 412 4664
www.breastfeedingnetwork.org.uk
*An independent source of
support and information,
answering FAQs and providing
fact sheets to help mothers
make informed choices.*

British Dietetic Association
5th Floor
Charles House
148-149 Great Charles Street
Queensway
Birmingham B3 3HT
Tel: 0121 2008080
www.bda.uk.com
*The professional association for
dietitians, providing practical
guidance to enable people to
make appropriate lifestyle and
food choices.*

British Nutrition Foundation
High Holborn House
52-54 High Holborn
London WC1V 6RQ
Tel: 020 7404 6504
www.nutrition.org.uk
*A useful site that provides
healthy eating information
and recipes.*

The Food Commission
94 White Lion Street
Islington
London N1 9PF
Tel: 020 7837 2250
www.foodcomm.org.uk
*Campaigns for safer, healthier
food in the UK. Website has a
very good links page, detailing
which organisations are most
likely to be of use for consumers
with specific questions.*

Food Standards Agency
Aviation House
125, Kingsway
London WC2B 6NH
Tel: 020 7276 8000
www.food.gov.uk
*Protects the public's health and
consumer interests. A useful
website for understanding food
labelling rules and regulations
relating to food manufacture
and production.*

Lakeland Limited
Alexandra Buildings
Windermere
Cumbria LA23 1BQ
Tel: 01539 488100
www.lakeland.co.uk
*Stockists of a vast range of
kitchen equipment.*

La Leche League
PO Box 29
West Bridgford
Nottingham NG2 7NP
Tel: 0845 456 1855
www.laleche.org.uk
*An organization to encourage
mother-to-mother support for
breastfeeding. Provides links to
your local group and the option
to become a member.*

Mothercare
Cherry Tree Road
Watford
Hertfordshire, WD24 6SH
Tel: 08453 304070
www.mothercare.com
*Stockists of a wide range of
feeding equipment.*

National Childbirth Trust (NTC)
Alexandra House
Oldham Terrace
London W3 6NH
Tel: 0870 4448707

www.nct.org.uk
*Local branches offer support for
parents and parents-to-be, and
organise various activities and
events in your area. The website
provides articles on a range of
topics and offers helplines for
parents' different needs,
including breastfeeding
counselling. There is also the
opportunity to subscribe to
egroups and an "Ask our
experts" feature.*

Vegan Society
Donald Watson House
21 Hylton Street
Hockley
Birmingham B18 6HJ
Tel: 0121 5231730
www.vegansociety.com
*Provides useful advice on
nutrtition, and bringing up
vegan children.*

Vegetarian Society
Parkdale, Dunham Road
Altrincham
Cheshire WA14 4GQ
Tel 0161 9252000
www.vegsoc.org
*Offers expert advice on
nutritional issues and provides
advice on recipes, approved
products, and eating out.*

your own useful addresses

Use these pages to record addresses and phone numbers that you may want to keep a note of, such as your doctor, midwife, or breastfeeding support group, as well as useful websites you may come across. It's handy to keep them all in one place.

Index

about the author

Annabel Karmel MBE is the leading author on nutrition and cooking for children and her bestselling books are sold all over the world. A mother of three, Annabel is well known for providing advice and guidance to millions of parents on what to feed their children, as well as getting families to eat a healthier diet without spending hours in the kitchen.

Annabel writes regularly for newspapers and magazines, and appears frequently on radio and TV as the UK's top expert on children's nutrition. She has several ranges of healthy ready meals in supermarkets based on her most popular recipes, including her *Eat Fussy* range for one to four year olds and her *Make It Easy* range. She has a distinctive range of equipment for preparing baby food. Annabel's balanced meals are now served in the leading theme parks in the UK, one of the leading nursery groups, and in the largest chain of family based holiday parks.

Her popular website www.annabelkarmel.com is the number one online destination for child nutrition, featuring advice, delicious recipes, and social networking.

acknowledgements

Author's Acknowledgements
I'd like to thank Peggy Vance at DK for making it such fun to work on this book; Caroline Stearns for working with me and testing all the yummy recipes, and her beautiful daughter Aurelia who once again is a cover model; Dave King for his stunning photos; Valerie Berry for her food styling; Elizabeth Jones for keeping my business running while I wrote this book; Evelyn Etkind, my mum, for tasting my recipes – even the baby purées!; Marina Magpoc Abaigar and Letty Catada for helping me in the kitchen; Mary Jones, my loyal publicist; Dr Alison French; Dr Adam Fox, Consultant Paediatric Allergist; all the models; and the wonderful team at DK: Helen Murray, Peggy Sadler, Sara Kimmins, Esther Ripley, and Marianne Markham.

Publisher's Acknowledgements
DK would like to thank Chloe Brown for prop styling; Dr Adam Fox, Consultant Paediatric Allergist at Guys' and St Thomas' Hospitals, for his invaluable allergy advice; Dr Rosan Meyer, Specialist Paediatric Dietitian at Imperial College, for checking the nutritional information with a limited amount of time; Susan Bosanko for the index; Alyson Silverwood for proofreading; Andrea Bagg, Nicola Parkin, and Karen Sullivan for editorial assistance; Charlotte Seymour for help on photo shoots, Robert Merret for additional help with prop styling; and our models: Lexie Benbow-Hart, Lachlan Bush, Gracie Daly, Georgina Davie, Ava Felton, Humaira Felton, Lewie Gunter, Dharminder Kang, Jas Kang, Zen Kang, Amais Limerick, Esther Marney, Ruben Morris, Ruby Read, Charlotte Seymour, Lizzie Shepherd, Aurelia Stearns, and Simona Tigîrlas.

Picture credits
The publisher would like to thank the following for their kind permission to reproduce their photographs:
(Key: b- bottom; l-left)
Corbis: Lou Chardonnay 28; John W. Gertz/zefa 8; Norbert Schaefer 21bl; PunchStock: Photodisc 84
All other images © Dorling Kindersley
For further information see: www.dkimages.com